The Woods Were Full of Men

Irma Lee Emmerson
with Jean Muir

Published by Echo Point Books & Media
Brattleboro, Vermont
www.EchoPointBooks.com

Copyright © 1963 Irma Lee Emmerson and Jean Muir

ISBN: 978-1-62654-071-2

Cover illustration by Noella Jackson

Cover design by Adrienne Núñez,
Echo Point Books & Media

Editorial and proofreading assistance by Christine Schultz,
Echo Point Books & Media

Printed and bound in the United States of America

TO THE LOGGERS

THE WOODS WERE FULL OF MEN

chapter one

WOMEN keep talking about the terrible dearth of unattached males. They tell me it is virtually impossible to find extra men for dinner parties. I find it difficult to work up any sympathy for their social problems. Sometimes I wonder how these frustrated hostesses would feel if they had been in my boots, with sixty extra men, most of them unattached, responding when dinner was announced. I know how I felt. I felt as if I were standing directly in the path of a herd of stampeding Percherons.

Now I am very fond of men. One man is wonderful. A few extra ones around to pass the cocktails can be pleasant and helpful. After that I draw the line. They eat too much. Twenty pies a day, for example. Three hundred pancakes. All in addition to their regular fodder.

I landed up in the big timber country of Oregon, the only woman among all those pie-eating, pancake-consuming men, as the result of a family conference which did not work out as planned.

A family conference can be a peculiarly painful thing. Especially when the family is made up of kindly people who are hell-bent on helping you at great inconvenience to themselves.

Unfortunately, at conferences of this kind, I was always the one my relatives wanted to help, being the impractical and unsuccessful member of a large, practical and successful

2

family. We had all gone out into the world from our parents' dairy farm in southern Oregon, my four sisters to make good and happy marriages, my three brothers to apply themselves to their worthy professions, and I to fall flat on my face.

My father used to say with pride, "My son-in-law, the admiral." Or, "My son, the professor." Or, "My daughter's husband, the doctor." When he came to me, he would pat my head affectionately and say, "Irma Lee, my fair-haired daughter." It is very trying to go through life with nothing distinctive about you except the fact that you have fair hair. Fair hair is quite commonplace among people of our background, which is English, Dutch and French Canadian on my father's side and Scotch Irish on my mother's. Yet for over thirty years that is all anybody could think of when they wanted to speak nicely about me.

The final conference to which I was subjected was a small one, involving only my sister Elva, her husband Ole, and me. The affair took place in their San Francisco apartment and concerned my announcement that I was going to find myself a job. After all, I had been living off them for several years and, as I pointed out, the time had come when I simply could not go on sponging.

Instantly my sister El plunged into a flattering account of how useful I was. The way she had it worked out, I actually saved them money by living there. Tactfully, she refrained from mentioning that anyway I probably could not get a job, my past efforts to establish myself having been remarkably unsuccessful. First I had thought I would be a nurse, but after I had staggered around with bedpans for months, I had been told with the utmost kindliness that perhaps I would be wise to go in for something which did not require so much physical stamina. Then I decided I would be a writer. By the most furious effort I produced seven full-length novels. El and Ole thought they were wonderful. Editors did not. By that time I really did not care. I was perfectly sure my beau, my handsome, brilliant and sophisticated beau, had serious matrimonial intentions. It turned out he had serious intentions, all right, but they were not matrimonial ones. At least, not so far as I was concerned. That, too, was a subject tactfully ignored at the conference. Ole and El, drowning out my feeble voice, went on with warm affection about how the household could not possibly get along without me.

This was all so much loving hog wash. At the moment Ole and El were having to scrimp. Ole was one of the fathers of the miniature X-ray program and a big man in the TB Association. He was a big man in more ways than one, standing six feet six in his stocking feet when he was able to stand at all. For months he had been laid up with TB himself, carrying on his work from his bed on a reduced salary.

As long as my sister El had been working I really had been useful. I would rouse my nephew Knute in the early morning to start him on his paper route, get breakfast, do the housework, answer the doorbell, serve coffee and coffee cake to Ole's callers and have dinner ready when El came home in the evening. But recently El had given up her job to spend more time with Ole and the last thing they needed was another mouth to feed.

"When you cook, you save more than the cost of what you eat," El kept insisting.

Ole had been lying with his eyes shut. All at once he opened them and sat up in his favorite position, Buddha-like, with the covers twisted around his waist. "You know, El," he said, sounding surprised, "I think Lee really wants a job." Then they both looked at me, very searchingly, as if they were trying to adjust themselves to the idea of the

4

eminently domestic Lee wanting to make money instead of coffee cake.

"I'd give my eyeteeth for one," I cried out and I think there must have been an hysterical urgency in my voice, because right there the conference stopped running true to type. Instead of bringing reasonable arguments to bear, Ole and El stopped looking at me and glanced instead at each other. Apparently some telepathic communication passed between them, because Ole reached for the telephone.

My brother-in-law was a virtuoso when it came to the phone. He used it so much, working from his bed, that he could play the thing like a violin. No matter what anybody wanted, Langlois blue cheese, tickets to a sold-out play or a pair of Siberian wolfhounds, when Ole picked up the phone these desirable things materialized.

By the time he finished talking to a Mr. Belton, he had the man convinced that what the architectural firm of Belton and Wicket needed most for the branch they were opening in San Francisco was an A-one receptionist. A receptionist's job was exactly the sort of thing my relatives thought suitable for me. The idea also strongly appealed to me. I had an invigorating picture of myself, speaking in well-modulated tones and being tactful to clients.

"An exceptionally pleasant girl, Mr. Belton," Ole was saying, "with a nice, honest smile—well, let's see. Five feet two. I'd say about 37-24-36—yes, isn't it?"

Family loyalty was getting a little the better of Ole. My waist was twenty-four inches only when I sucked in my breath and grew black in the face.

"She'll be there Monday morning at nine thirty for her test. Thank you, too, sir. Good-bye." He looked over at me with the complacent expression of a man who has just landed a ten-pound trout. "Well, there's your receptionist job, Sis."

There, from my point of view, was felicity. Except for one small detail. It appeared that tact and a well-modulated voice were not the only qualities Belton and Wicket expected from a receptionist. They also expected some typing skill.

"Just a little typing," Ole said, as if it were of no significance. "Just a letter now and then when the stenographers are busy."

I had done a great deal of typing while producing all those manuscripts. But I had done it slowly and messily. I do not have fine typist's hands. My hands are the square kind with unusually chubby thumbs. Personally I am very fond of my thumbs. When I am worried, I look at them and the sight of those little fat thumbs steadies me. They look indomitable. But for typing I could get along just as well with my toes.

"Well," Ole said, "you've got until Monday to practice. They only require forty words a minute."

So there it was. My big chance. From that Friday until Sunday night I typed. I set up my typewriter in the laundry room so as not to drive the family wild and typed until my head throbbed, my back ached and my fingers felt like fat frankfurters dangling from my wrists. And by late Sunday afternoon, when I coaxed my nephew Knute away from his model planes long enough to clock me, I was hitting forty words a minute. I even reached forty-five once or twice. At about that time, Ole sent down word to me that I was to stop this nonsense and go to bed or I would look like hell for my interview.

After a good ten hours' sleep I faced the new day with the greatest confidence. I brushed my hair until it shone

6

and used restraint with makeup. And as I set out for the streetcar, the sight of El, Ole and Knute all waving encouragement from the window made me feel that, with very little effort, I would have the business world actually crawling on its belly before me. That is, until I got downtown and found myself outside the building where Belton and Wicket had their offices. Then I panicked.

I remembered to stand still and breathe deeply for a few minutes to regain my senses before I marched in, trying to imagine I had a book on my head. I came through the inquisition fairly well. The trouble started when Mr. Belton handed me over to a terribly stylish and intelligent-looking older woman for the typing test. All at once I could not even remember the keyboard. While I shoved paper into the infernal machine and the woman arranged a letter on a rack for me to copy, I kept mumbling to myself, "a,s,d,f,g—" and there my mind went blank. Well, I thought, maybe my fingers will do it of their own accord.

I made my forty words a minute, all right. Unfortunately I wrote "personal" instead of "personnel" and transposed the "i" and the "e" in "received." This jolted me so badly that my right hand got off base for an entire sentence and "We would be glad to hear from you," came out looking like some cryptic message written by a dangerously subversive alien.

From force of habit I caught the Taraval streetcar and slumped down in a seat. No doubt back-fence psychologists would tell me that the reason I failed to notice when we reached my street was that, subconsciously, I could not bear to go home and face El and Ole in my defeated condition.

"You all right, Miss?" the conductor asked me.

"Why, yes," I said, sitting up straighter, "I'm fine." For

7

the first time I noticed that the streetcar had reached the end of the line.

"You'll have to pay again if you're going back," the conductor said.

"Oh no, I'm getting off," I told him, jumping up and charging toward the door. I headed straight for the gateway to Fleishacker Zoo, because it happened to be handy. I'll go and talk to the apes, I thought. I should feel right at home.

For an hour I wandered around staring gloomily at the animals. Finally I flopped onto a long bench opposite monkey island. By that time I had decided failure was basic with me. There I was, no man in my life and rejected by the business world. At the moment I could not think of one good thing I had done in my life. No doubt peacocks were screaming, lions were roaring and monkeys were chittering around me. I heard none of them. The only thing that cut through the clouds of self-pity which engulfed me were the words "Coos Bay."

Those words will bring me wide awake out of the soundest sleep. The dairy farm near Coos Bay, Oregon, where I was brought up, had long since been sold. My father had retired and he and Mother lived further north, near Portland. Just the same, some inner part of me always thinks that Coos Bay is home. My mind knows it isn't. But my heart does not. So I turned around to see who was talking.

Two tall men were sitting at the other end of my bench. They lounged at ease with a noticeable lack of city tension about them. Each man wore slacks of heavy, green gabardine topped by a square-cut jacket of the same material. Their brown oxfords were highly polished and their soft fedoras looked expensive. From my childhood I remembered seeing timber cruisers and loggers doing the town dressed like that.

"Funny how those monkeys look like people you know, isn't it?" the taller of the two men said.

"Yep," the other one answered. "That little one on the stump. High, bald forehead, ears sticking straight out. Ain't that a ringer for Swivelneck?"

"Damned if he ain't."

I had a feeling the taller of the two knew he had an audience. I turned my head, but not before I had seen the flash of water-green eyes that made me think of a fractious horse. As I listened, I gathered both men were attending a meeting of the I.W.A., which I supposed meant International Woodworkers of America.

"And why the hell the men voted us in as delegates, I'll never know," the man at the far end of the bench said. "I'd rather be blowing stumps or chasing cat for you anytime."

"Aw, quit griping, Ed. You were making plenty hay last night with that doll you picked up on the plane."

"Me? As if any dame even knew I was alive when the famous Wild Bill Moran is percolating."

The name "Wild Bill" certainly suited the green-eyed, devil-may-care logger next to me, I thought.

"Hell, you didn't want her anyway," he said.

The one called Ed chuckled. "How'd you know? You dope, trying to get her to go to camp! If she ever hit Ticoma, Old Fox would take one look and smell trouble."

"He'd try to drag her out in the brush if he was smart. Heck, he's been howling for a second cook, hasn't he? And you can't say I didn't tempt her. Four fifty plus room and board ain't hay for any doll."

"And when you said she'd see you every night, I don't see how she could resist."

"That's a mystery to me, too," Wild Bill said.

I hardly heard the last two sentences. The words, "Four fifty plus room and board ain't hay for any doll," were echoing and reechoing through my head like horns on New Year's Eve. FOUR FIFTY! I thought, stunned. And for a second cook!

"I guess we'd better push off," I heard Ed say. "We've got some more speeches to listen to at two."

They got up to leave, two tall, sunburned men who looked as if they had done a great deal of vigorous scrubbing behind their ears. Just as they came opposite me, the one called Ed glanced down at me. There was a remarkably candid look about his face and his eyes were of the unbelievable blue the sky sometimes gets on a late June twilight. He smiled and I thought, homesick all at once, that's the way they've always smiled in Coos Bay. Even at strangers.

They walked away with the free-swinging, lordly stride of woodsmen, and suddenly it seemed to me I had been listening to the voices of a pair of angels who had materialized to point out the path of destiny. If there was one thing in the world I could do it was cook.

The two green-clad figures were disappearing among the trees and I had a wild impulse to shout, "Hey, wait for me." Then I slumped back again, realizing that to sensible people, the idea of kiting off to Oregon as the result of a conversation overheard on a zoo bench would seem the height of idiocy. Yet, there the idea was, full blown in my mind. And thinking it over, in my own squirrely way, I could not see that it was idiotic at all. Up in a logging camp called Ticoma, a person named Old Fox was howling for a second cook. I needed a job and I could cook. The only real money I had made in the last few years was working for a caterer. Not, I realized, that I could feed loggers hors d'oeuvres, canapés and dainty sandwiches, such as I had been making for pink teas and cocktail parties.

What on earth do loggers eat I asked myself and immediately thought, with an upsurge of confidence, of apple pies and hot cakes. I know a trick or two with hot cakes, and the fact that the town involved was Coos Bay made the whole affair seem perfectly respectable and reasonable.

I glanced down at my hands and saw they were looking wonderfully competent. Just get those chubby little thumbs into a mess of pie dough and they knew exactly what they were intended to do in life.

I had made up my mind to go to Oregon and be a cook in a logging camp even before I realized that it would have the added advantage of getting me away from the telephone. Recently, during all my waking hours, I had been keeping one ear cocked for the phone, particularly between the critical evening hours of five thirty and nine. I would not even go to a movie at night for fear I might miss a call. This morbid attitude had started three weeks before when I opened the morning paper and discovered that Doug Weatherby, my beau, had got himself engaged to another girl. At first I did not believe a word of it. I kept expecting him to call and explain that the whole thing was some silly mistake on the part of the society department.

I suppose the man just did not like explanations. Or maybe he expected me to call him and offer hearty congratulations. In either case, I had not heard a word from him since. And after three weeks nothing ever happens. But at least, I told myself, jumping up, I could shake the dust of San Francisco off my feet.

It was only eight blocks to the apartment. When I arrived, out of breath and buoyant, I discovered that no one was home except Knute who came up from the basement and told me the family had gone downtown for Ole's X ray.

"Well," I said breezily, "I flopped. But it doesn't matter because I've got a much better job lined up. Second cook in a logging camp in Coos Bay."

Clearly this sounded as magnificent to Knute as it did to me. "Wow," he breathed and let out a long, admiring whistle.

I did not feel it necessary to explain that the only lining up I had done was to overhear a conversation at the zoo.

"Gosh, Aunt Lee," he said, in an awed voice, "could you fix me up with a job next summer?"

"I don't know why not," I told him.

"Oh, man," Knute said. But apparently a second thought presented itself just then because he added, looking uncertain, "Mom'll have a fit when she hears you're going to a logging camp."

"She will, won't she?" I said, equally uneasy all at once.

Our glances met. "Maybe you'd better get started before they come back," Knute suggested.

Immediately I surged into action. "Call the bus station. Find out how much it costs and when the next bus leaves." Tearing into my room, I pulled bags and hat box out of the closet.

The fare came to $13.30 plus ten percent tax and the bus left in two hours. When I dumped the contents of my purse onto the bed I found I had exactly $15.89.

"Gosh, Aunt Lee," Knute said, "that doesn't leave you much to eat on."

"So? Who wants to eat?" I started shoving sweaters, jeans and wool skirts into my valise. Then I added my cotton dresses, every pair of low-heeled shoes I owned and,

12

after a moment's consideration, my new and seductive dinner gown.

We left the apartment like sailboats scudding before the oncoming storm. At the station Knute checked my bags through to Coos Bay and shook hands, since he was too old for kissing aunts. There was a curiously self conscious expression on his face, mixed with a funny little pride which I could not understand at all, until he dropped a handful of change into my suit pocket. "For coffee and stuff," he said.

I knew it came from his paper route. It probably meant the sacrifice of the model plane he wanted, but I swallowed my protests after one look at his face and managed not to disgrace him by growing tearful. "I'm going to miss you, fella," I said and dived into the bus.

The seat next to mine was empty, which I took to be a good omen. The very day itself seemed full of promises as we rolled up through California—a warm June day, all ready for adventure. When we reached the redwoods there was still a glimmer of light left, enough to lend a mysterious quality to the deep shadows. I had rather recklessly rented a pillow with some of Knute's money so I kicked off my high-heeled pumps and curled up in the double seat. I would doze off, wake again with a sense of blissful freedom and once more drop asleep, murmuring, "'There is a tide in the affairs of men, which, taken at the flood, leads on to fortune.'"

I had a cup of coffee and a doughnut at midnight and toast and coffee in a little coast town at daybreak. The Californians must have left the bus at their various destinations along the way. Sitting at the counter, I felt sure my fellow travelers were now Oregonians. They were not a particularly exciting or stylish-looking group but there was a nicely competent look about them, as if they all felt very much at home in the world. A remark a brother-in-law once made flashed through my mind. He said, "You can always spot an Oregonian. When you tell him anything he'll say, 'That's what I hear.' Then there will be a weighty pause and he'll add, 'But I don't believe it.'"

"All right, folks," the bus driver said. As we began paying our checks, a man looked up from his paper. "It says here the price of lumber's going up ten percent by fall," he said.

"So I hear," another one answered. There was a pause and I held my breath. "But I don't believe it," he added and we all looked at him with quiet approval and climbed back onto the bus. Then I *knew* I was home.

I could not sleep after we reached Coos County. The ocean, the rivers and creeks, the low morning fog that hid the miraculous greenness were themselves like some lovely, familiar dream to me. I thought that even in the stuffy bus I could smell the pungent aroma of waxy myrtle trees.

We were due in Coos Bay at eight. Since the lumber office was apt to be a good distance from the bus depot I surreptitiously counted my change. It came to two dollars and a quarter. I decided I would eat up the quarter and hope the two dollars would get me to the office.

As we neared the bay I could see lumber mills crouched on every likely spot. When I had left there had been only two or three. Now there seemed to be dozens. The bus pulled up before a low brick building not far from the main street and I was the first one out, sniffing the sharp, pitchy odor of Douglas fir and Port Orford cedar and the saltiness of the sea in the morning fog.

The lumber office, I suspected, would not be open before eight thirty. And right then, as I pictured myself walking

14

in to apply for the job, I felt my confidence deflating like a punctured tire. The chances were ten to one there would be no job. With awful clarity I realized the trip had been prompted only by wishful thinking. Even if this logging company did want a second cook, they would certainly expect some recommendations—they weren't going to hire a pig in a poke. Probably I would have to telephone El, collect, and ignominiously ask her to wire money for my return fare.

I crawled into the rest room and stared disconsolately at my own face in the glass while I combed my hair and washed up. It was a nice face, I thought, and deserved a better fate than to be stuck with a fool like Irma Lee Emmerson for life. The grey-green eyes were hopeful eyes and seemed to expect nice things to happen instead of one ignominy after another.

The cab which I had noticed parked at the curb when we arrived had left when I came out so I sat dejectedly in the lunchroom, spending my quarter on coffee and doughnuts and trying to revive my courage. "How much to take me to the Ticoma Lumber Company?" I asked the driver when he returned.

"Ticoma! You mean it, lady?" He peered at me suspiciously from under his cap, fat faced and red eyed. "That'd cost you thirty dollars."

My dismayed expression seemed to irritate him further. "Well, it's fifty-five miles," he said belligerently. "Nobody takes a cab up there except a bunch of drunken loggers."

"But the town office! Don't they have a town office?" My lips were trembling so I could hardly talk.

"Oh, you mean the Coos Pacific? Well, that's only a dollar and a half. Ticoma is their logging camp."

I climbed into the cab, still feeling shaken. As he pulled

away from the curb I decided I would tip him my last fifty cents, for luck.

He drove along the waterfront. The fog was beginning to lift and I could see the fishing fleet tied up along the old riverboat docks. Apparently the fish were not running, even though it was turning into a warm summer day. Further on we passed big lumber schooners and Japanese marus berthed by the docks where piles of logs were cold decked. Then the cab pulled up in front of a long building beside a dock. I climbed out and stood for a moment in front of a white clapboard office. Blue hydrangeas lined its front and a gravel path cut across a patch of grass to its door. Somewhere in the background saws were whining and the odor of pitchy lumber tickled my nostrils.

chapter two

WHEN applying for a job, I had always understood that you had to answer a great many nosy questions about personal things, such as your age and your marital status and whether or not you had any terrible neuroses. Mr. Knowland at the Coos Pacific was not interested in any of these things.

He was a short man, built like a bull, with grey hair growing low on his forehead and a pair of remarkably shrewd blue eyes. When the girl at the front desk showed me into his office, he reared back a little from his desk and said, "The girl tells me you're looking for a second cook's job."

His glance swept over me and stopped at my feet in their high-heeled pumps. I looked down, too, and noticed with dismay that I was standing pigeon toed. "Got any other shoes?" he asked.

"Why yes," I began, carefully turning my toes out again. "My bags—"

"Four fifty a month," he cut in. "Twelve days on, two days off. Friday afternoon till Sunday evening. No monkeyshines. Okay?"

I just stood there gaping at him. Then I saw he expected me to say something. "Okay, Mr. Knowland," I stammered.

"Just call me Old Fox. Everybody else does." He planted his hands on his desk and heaved himself to his feet. His eyes were exactly on a level with my own. Up to this point there had been a barely restrained elation in his manner. But all at once those eyes of his narrowed alarmingly. In fact, he looked extremely tough altogether. "You'll be the only gal in camp. I hope you're a lady," he said in a most meaningful way.

My startled expression seemed to reassure him. "All right, all right," he roared. "So you're a lady. So let's go."

And just like that I was no longer among the unemployed. It was almost *too* precipitate. He herded me out the door as if I were a skittish heifer that might try to make a break for it. After he stopped the dusty old pickup by the bus station and came out again with my bags, I could have sworn there was a relieved expression on his face when he saw me still sitting there.

"I suppose you can cook?" he asked as we jounced along the river road and then gave a bellow of laughter at the tardiness of that vital question.

By this time I had come out of my stunned condition and was asking myself a searching question. Just what was so horrible about the well-paying job of second cook at the Ticoma logging camp? It must be something particularly dreadful or Old Fox would not have been in such a tearing hurry to get me out of town. Not even asking for references. It was more like shanghaiing than hiring.

I glanced nervously at Old Fox. Cetrainly he looked like a reliable man. He had nice furrows at the corners of his ice-blue eyes and I liked the vital look of his grey hair. I even liked his authoritative manner. Nobody, after talking two minutes to Old Fox, would think of him as a small man. I leaned back in the seat, aware that I had been sitting bolt upright, every nerve tense.

At first low-hanging clouds concealed most of the valley,

but before long bordering hills rose above the fog. It is the greenest landscape in the world, dark green of Douglas firs covering the hills, lighter green of lush meadows. One pasture looked like a miniature lake, the fog that covered it so shallow that the heads of the Jersey cows seemed to float there, as if it were a translucent sea.

When we reached the spot where the north fork spilled into the main river the water began babbling to me about home and I caught my breath. In the distance I could see the old home ranch. Not a soul I knew lived there now, or had for years and yet I felt an irrational impulse to leap out of the car. For that instant it seemed to me I could run across those dearly familiar meadows straight back into my childhood, back to the old house with the family atmosphere closing protectively around me, instead of sitting here and being driven off into something alarmingly unknown.

Well, anyway, I have a job, I told myself. I didn't believe it. The transition had been so swift that nothing seemed in the least real, not the country, the ride with Old Fox or my prospects. I just sat there, quietly bouncing along with the pickup, feeling as if I had no relation to myself at all.

The road stayed on top of the dyke for miles. The tide was coming in I knew, because I could see bits of debris floating upstream. The myrtles and alders growing close to the water looked as if they had been bottom trimmed by the rise and fall of the tides. Finally the valley narrowed until it was only a ledge along one side of the river and riffles began to appear, so I knew we were leaving sea level and climbing into the mountains.

"Better take a good look at these shacks in Greenwood," Old Fox's voice said beside me. "You won't see another house for thirty-five miles."

19

Then the houses were past and there was nothing but trees. Huge Douglas firs grew almost to the water's edge, the underbrush pierced by shafts of morning sunlight. Huckleberry and salal were thick under the trees and rhododendron bushes grew twenty feet high, splashing the greenness with big coral-pink blossoms. Sometimes a little white stream raced under a covered bridge, and once Old Fox stopped the pickup so that I could watch a herd of elk. I counted thirty-five of them walking single file up the mountain, their great racks of horns vanishing over the skyline. The further we climbed, the higher the mountains grew. Now and then we could see outcroppings of rock, moss covered, through the solid banks of trees. There seemed to be dozens of waterfalls, reduced by summer's dryness to a misty spray, so that I would look up and see rainbows against the cliffs above me.

Big trees, several feet in diameter, clung tenaciously to their perches on these dark crags. Old Fox told me the only soil under these trees was often their own accumulation of decades, fir needles, decaying moss, crumbled limbs pruned by wind and time and dirt washed down from above. He said some of the hills near camp were just mountains of shale and the very devil to log. Trees there, he said, sometimes had root systems only a couple of feet in depth, making them dangerous to fell even though they grew so straight grained and tall. "It's hard to keep your footing up there. Take a step and you land in a waterhole. The place is full of springs seeping up through the shale."

Two and a half hours after leaving the bay we rattled across a wooden bridge and came in sight of the camp, sprawling in an easy bend of the Ticoma just below where it met the east fork of the Coila River. A row of tar-papered bunkhouses backed up against the foot of a hill. They had

20

obviously been moved there full grown, set on the bias as they were, so tip-tilted I wondered how the men could keep their footing. The campsite looked triangular, the sides of the triangle formed by the two rivers and its base by the steep hill.

The car jolted across another bridge, swung past a flat stretch of ground where some trucks were parked and pulled up by the porch of the cookhouse, our dust overtaking us in a great cloud.

At the insistent blast of the horn, two men rushed out of the door. In the lead was a fat, bald man with alarmingly aggressive eyebrows. The man directly behind him was tall, lean and younger, in his mid-thirties, I guessed. Since they came out of the cookhouse and both wore white aprons, I stared up at them anxiously, knowing they were going to be very, very important to me from now on.

"Come on, gal, out with you," Old Fox said, holding open the door of the pickup. Over his shoulder, he said to the two men on the steps, "Brought you a second cook." There was no mistaking the satisfaction in his voice, like a man who has just pulled off a very slick deal. The reaction of the two men was equally obvious. It was incredulous delight.

Good heavens, I thought wildly, has the camp run out of food? Do they *eat* second cooks?

Old Fox shepherded me up the steps and into the cookhouse, the two men falling back before us. The cook and my immediate superior was the fat one whom Old Fox introduced as Meatball. The thin one was John Paul, dishwasher and flunkey. I was relieved to see that in spite of Meatball's ferocious eyebrows, he did not look at all like the crabby old cook I had pictured. I thought he had quite a kindly expression.

21

It was apparent that all three men were waiting with some pride for my reaction to the cookhouse, so I glanced about in what I hoped was a professional manner. I had never been in a cookhouse before, but this one looked brand new, spotless and efficient. A fifteen-foot stove with a six-foot grill was backed up against the far wall. Within easy reach was a serving counter, a double-decked affair with stacks of dishes on the top shelf. I also noticed two walk-in freezers with a storeroom between. To the left of the stove, a waist-high counter stretched twenty feet along one wall, below a solid row of windows. I later learned the counter was called a "pieboard." Twin, four-foot sinks with a draining shelf above formed an island between pastry works and stove, making it easy, I could see, for the cooks to toss kettles into the waiting soapy water. There was also a triple-sink unit near a door which I saw led into the dining room.

Beyond the door I could see about a dozen rough-board tables, covered with green linoleum and flanked by long benches. But the thing which really caught my eye was a rough sign above the doorway. In letters half a foot high were the words: COWS MAY COME AND COWS MAY GO BUT THE BULL GOES ON FOREVER.

The men were still waiting expectantly so I spoke with admiration of the arrangements and they looked gratified.

"Just wait until all the new buildings are finished," Old Fox said. "We'll have the slickest camp in the country. The men's dormitory is something revolutionary in logging camps. Fifty double rooms with a bath between each two rooms. Neatest little cabins for the kitchen crew. But in the meantime I'll have to stable you in the Old Homestead."

The noon meal was over but Meatball rustled us up a

22

lunch and then we all set out for the Old Homestead in procession, the dust spurting under our feet. Old Fox led with my vanity case, followed by John Paul carrying my fortnighter and Meatball, carrying a bag in each hand, paunch sedately preceding him. He would have looked terribly dignified if his apron had not been accidentally hitched up so that, as I brought up the rear, in his hind pocket I could see a paperback book with the unlikely title, *The Gentle Love of Susy Swann*.

At first I thought we were heading for the row of lop-sided bunkhouses, but instead we stopped short of them at a shack just above the river. "And this," Old Fox said, "is your private castle."

Well, it was a most deplorable-looking habitation. Above the furrowed door was a time-bleached set of antlers and under them, burned into the wood, the inscription: Amos Lange—1905.

The shack itself was made of hand-hewn cedar, its jutting beams still showing the grooved bite of the adze. The shake siding was grey with age and a dexterous cat could have jumped through the cracks. John Paul leaned his shoulder against the door and shoved. It groaned open. "It will take a bit of tidying up," Old Fox said, watching me covertly as I stopped at the top of the rickety steps. That was the wildest understatement of the year. I was looking into the abandoned lair of some carefree logger. There were piles of rotted clothing, stacks of mice-riddled papers, discarded calk boots and tobacco cans all over the splintered floor.

"Four fifty, plus room and board," I muttered to myself and managed a rather spiritless smile.

"Where's Snoozy? Where's that lazy bull cook?" Old Fox demanded.

"Probably sleeping it off in the sheethouse," John Paul said.

"Well, rustle him up to help this little lady get settled," Old Fox told him.

"Maybe we'd better leave her gear on the porch. This place stinks," he added as he barged off.

John Paul wandered away, presumably to find the bull cook (whatever that was), in the sheethouse, which I supposed must be a place where bed linens and extra blankets were stored. I was left standing on the porch with Meatball, who folded his hands over his big stomach and smiled down at me benevolently. He told me not to bother about a thing that afternoon, since he had the supper well under control. If I came to the cookhouse at three thirty, he said, we would all go swimming. And in the meantime he suggested I take a nap. The nap habit, he said, was something I had better learn, since I would have to get up at four every morning to help with the breakfast.

While he talked I was conscious of huffling sounds below the shack which grew into loud snuffles and honks when he stepped off the porch. As he proceeded back toward the cookhouse, a matronly looking sow squeezed out from under the shack and went trotting hurriedly after him. Instantly a great squealing broke out and half a dozen pigs came scurrying out and fell in line behind her. I watched the picturesque little parade out of sight and then, somewhat squeamishly, inspected my new home.

The back windows looked down on the river and a cool, flickering riffle. So far, so good. Just outside a flimsy door I discovered a typical old-fashioned privy. Above the hole, at eye level, some noble son of Paul Bunyan had pasted a printed sign now yellow with age:

24

> In days of old, when men were bold,
> Ere paper was invented,
> Men wiped their rump on a piece of stump,
> And walked away contented.

I was back in the shack, standing disconsolately in the center of the mess, when Snoozy, the bull cook, arrived, an elderly little man who looked me over with bulging, inquisitive eyes. His lower lip protruded so alarmingly that at first I thought he must have a French fried potato squirreled away there until it became obvious it was a wad of snoose. He had a noticeable bun on and began at once to complain about his "bumlago." Yet within five minutes, I felt as if I had opened a bottle and a wonderful little old jinn had appeared.

He insisted I stay on the porch and rest myself while he carried out armloads of junk and burned it in a screen-covered barrel, attacked cobwebs with his broom and swept out the spiders. While all this furious activity went on, I sat collapsed on a circular wooden slab worn smooth by generations of sprawling loggers. Even so I could feel slivers through my seat. I was too tired and sleepy to care. It had turned into a blazing hot day and I would have thought the whole little valley was deserted except for the steady rapping of hammers down by the river.

"You're sure lucky," Snoozy called out. "That last joker who was here put in a cold-water pipe from the spring so you won't have to pack water."

I had supposed that a bull cook must have something to do with cooking. But Snoozy told me his job was to make the men's beds, sweep out their bunkhouses and build their fires in the late afternoon during rainy weather so they could dry out their clothes. The name was just a hangover from the old days when the bull cook kept the kitchen fire going and took the men's hot lunches to the woods at noon. The men carried their lunches in pails nowadays, he said, and only the bosses ate their noon dinner in the cookhouse.

After he had scrubbed out my new mansion with lye water, he set off for the sheethouse to rustle up what he optimistically described as my furniture. This consisted of a cot with tired springs, a pad which looked as if it had escaped from a Goodwill truck, a stand threatening to collapse with every squeak, and three wooden orange crates. Snoozy stacked the crates on top of each other, nailed the contraption to the wall and said it was a chest. Well, I thought, if I tack a piece of cretonne to the front, at least I'll have a place to hide my panties.

Above the chest, Snoozy fastened a mirror. I took one look at myself in it and backed hurriedly off. The mirror was cracked and wavy and made me look exactly like Pa's old bird dog.

There were also a number of empty powder boxes—and that meant blasting powder, not face powder. Without powder boxes, I gathered, a logging camp could not run. They were used for chairs, night stands, cupboards and under-the-bed chests.

By this time the shack had begun to look quite livable. Snoozy drove nails on each side of one corner, fastened a wire between them and hung a sheet on it, to make a wardrobe. Fortunately, I had brought some clothes hangers. As I unpacked the fortnighter and hung up my dresses, Snoozy tacked flour sacks over the windows. No two of them were exactly alike, but they were all gaily printed and I was surprised to see how cheerful they looked.

"You better ask Old Fox for a better mattress," Snoozy

said. "This one ain't fit for a flea-bitten dog." And with that comforting remark, he made off.

I dropped at once into a coma of exhaustion. So much had happened to me in the last twenty-four hours that I was not feeling anything except numbness. And yet the sensational developments of the day began after the alarm clock roused me. Still groggy with sleep, I climbed into my blue satin bathing suit. It was not new but the disenchanting mirror gave back some assurance that the curves were in approximately the proper places. Plodding sleepily along, the hot dust tickling my toes, I was halfway to the cookhouse to join Meatball and John Paul for our swim before I realized the crew was in from the woods.

Half a dozen high-backed trucks with rows of seats facing each other rolled across the bridge—crummies, I heard they were called. They pulled up and started disgorging loads of tired, dusty loggers. There was the cheerful sound of banter back and forth and the ring of lunch buckets above the tread of calk boots on the wooden walk. And then, as the men caught sight of me, a sudden incredulous silence. Not a whistle. Not a wolf call. Just a flat, dead silence. To my horror, I saw that some of the men actually turned their heads to look *away* from me.

I could feel my face flaming. There was no place to duck, either. I had to keep walking straight ahead, with that horrible silence all around me. I felt exactly like the woman taken in adultery.

When I finally burst into the cookhouse, even Meatball and John Paul backed off a step at sight of me. "Oh, what have I done?" I wailed, standing there in what now seemed to me to be my nakedness.

Meatball was the first to rally. "I guess I should have told you," he said, trying to be polite and not look at me too hard. "Any girl we have up here, Old Fox says she's supposed to cover up when she walks to the swimming hole."

"He thought I had more sense than to make a show of myself," I said miserably. Then I burst out, "What are they anyway? A bunch of monks?"

"Hardly." Meatball gave a snort. "But some of them don't get to town only every two or three months."

Actually Meatball was a horrible sight himself. All he had on was a pair of swimming trunks which left an awful lot of rolling fat in evidence.

"Forget it," he said, putting on a man-of-the-world expression. "The boys need a little treat once in a while."

That was the first intimation I had of the curious system of manners and morals in logging camps. These loggers operated right back in the golden days of the Old West. At least as far as women were concerned; floozies could have a whale of a time dancing on barroom tables in long black stockings, but the little woman at home kept her golden curls hidden behind a sunbonnet and forded rivers with her skirts pinned modestly down to her shoe tops. If you worked at the Ticoma logging camp, in the eyes of the loggers, you represented the little woman at home and you had just better act like it. Well, the camp was the only home a good many of those men had.

"The launching of Lee Emmerson," I groaned. "Better if you had busted a bottle of champagne over my rump." Following Meatball and John Paul I scrambled dejectedly down the bank to the swimming hole behind the cookhouse. Even the sight of the pool did not cheer me up much. It lay calm and lovely in the confluence of the two rivers, sheltered by alders and aromatic myrtles that grew almost to the waterline, their naked roots thrusting out into the pool.

28

Meatball bobbed about like some huge, blown-up rubber beach toy. I looked at John Paul a little askance. He had a good build, in a tall, lean way, but above his wrists and from his neckline to his waist he was one solid mass of tattoos. Sailing ships and American flags. Rose vines twined around his arms. Daggers and anchors and mermaids. On his chest, around which all the other whimsies grouped themselves, was a scroll, supported by four fat cupids with the name "Agnes" done in fine Spencerian letters.

John Paul kept watching me uneasily as I looked at all these things, as if he wanted to make sure I admired rather than disapproved. "Are you a seafaring man?" I asked, trying to sound bright and appreciative.

"Fifteen years," he said with a light-blue sideways glance at me, as if he had some portentous tale to tell. Reticence seemed to overtake him, though, because instead of telling it, he dived like an eel under water and I was left looking at the soles of a pair of big, pink feet.

When we finally left the pool, I skirted along the river bank, swimming part of the way, and skulked up the path which led to the back of the Old Homestead. Up to this point I had certainly been given the velvet-glove treatment, but the moment had now arrived when I was going to have to get over there and cook. Firmly I pushed back the picture which kept presenting itself to my mind, the picture of the cookhouse, full of black smoke from a burning supper and me being driven back in tears to Coos Bay by a disgusted Old Fox, while sixty outraged loggers cursed me on my way.

I prepared myself with great care, combing and pushing my wet hair into shape and putting on my prettiest pink cotton dress. Then I looked down at my two chubby thumbs for a final reassurance and set out. As I walked sedately along the rough walk, I had a strong feeling that I was under observation. Only this time my eyes were demurely on my toes. Still, it was a relief to enter the hot kitchen and face up to the supper.

Meatball was busy seasoning two big pans of potatoes which he called French bakes. My own first job was to make the biscuits. Fortunately, a slip with the required amounts was tacked to the wall, because I did not have the foggiest notion how many biscuits sixty hungry loggers could eat. I never did find out. I doubt if there are that many biscuits in the world.

Throwing myself into the task with a frenzied determination, I managed to get two baking sheets filled and ready for the oven and then I stood back and looked at them with admiration. There were over two hundred and they looked neat and professional. Modestly I carried them over and presented them to Meatball, hoping he would exclaim with pleasure at the sight. He hardly glanced at them. That they might not be good apparently had not occurred to him.

After that I made French dressing for the green salad John Paul was tossing in a stainless steel bowl big enough to take a bath in. I had thought John Paul was a deliberate man, but he was going at the job with a wonderful economy of motion, tearing lettuce into bite-size pieces, chopping celery, separating big white onions into rings, cutting up tomatoes and cucumbers. The cucumbers startled me. It was early for them. The last one I had bought in San Francisco cost thirty-nine cents. I began to suspect loggers lived pretty high on the hog.

When the bowl was in the walk-in freezer ready for the dressing to be added at the last minute, I had a look under the lids of the kettles on the stove. In one five-gallon kettle, giving off a fine aroma, were navy beans with hambones.

The other one held spinach just beginning to steam. Meatball slid my biscuits into the oven and it was time to start frying steaks, great T-bones that looked big enough to milk.

"When we get eight steaks on each platter, we'll ring the bell and fry the refills while they eat," Meatball said, as we tossed the steaks onto the smoking and slightly greased grill.

"You don't mean some of them eat more than one steak?" I asked, aghast.

"Most of them. Powder Box Pete can eat three T-bones or seven pork chops."

After that stupefying remark, there was only the sound of sizzling fat as we turned steaks, the perspiration running into our eyes. No wonder everybody was so happy to find a second cook, I thought. Poor Meatball and John Paul obviously had had their backs right up against the wall, trying to keep at bay sixty of the hugest appetites in Christendom. No doubt they would have welcomed me with open arms if I couldn't do anything but peel potatoes.

John Paul was whipping about, carrying bread and butter, pitchers of milk and cream, and the bowls of salad into the dining room. Steaks and biscuits would go on the table after the men were seated, but he lugged the great kettles and pans of French bakes over to the counter, and when most of the steaks were done I helped him fill serving bowls and carry them to the tables.

"You ought to watch this, Lee," Meatball called out. "It's a sight to warm any cook's heart." Smiling complacently he sailed out the door with me trailing along behind.

On the porch he took up a dignified stance behind a triangle made of tempered steel bars about a foot and a half long, hanging from a beam. With somewhat the air of a symphony conductor about to lead off, he raised an overgrown spike and began striking each bar in rapid succession. It made a curious sound, a cross between a church bell and some jungle rhythm. The sound seemed to invigorate him. He banged away with gusto, adding some deft flourishes. But by that time, I was not listening.

At the first chime, the doors of the bunkhouses flew open as if a hand had been poised over every doorknob and men erupted from the cabins. Sixty strong they came stampeding toward us. Meatball heard my gasp and called out over the chiming, "If one happens to fall down, he'll get up muttering, 'Too late now,' and go back to the bunkhouse." At the moment I almost believed the yarn.

I do not think any woman can stand still and see sixty men charging wildly toward her without experiencing a sort of primitive dismay. Without any volition on my part, I discovered I had nipped back into the kitchen. But I kept on watching.

The men entered the dining room in single file, walking eagerly, each with a quick glance toward the kitchen, fallers and buckers and high climbers, cat skinners and cat chasers, donkey punchers, whistle punks and choker setters. Every man seemed to have his own place which he took without hesitation at the tables set for eight. All of them had obviously changed their clothes. Their hair was slicked down with water, their faces freshly shaven. But there were none of the bright plaid shirts and nifty hiking pants I had seen in the movies. Most of them wore clean jeans and a blue or grey work shirt. A few were in slacks and sports shirts.

They lit into the supper with vigorous approval and little talking. All I could hear was pass this, pass that, or "short stop." "Short stop" meant a man was going to help himself before passing a dish along the line to someone who had asked for it.

32

Even at that first meal I could appreciate what a godsend it was to cook for men who responded so swiftly and enthusiastically to the dinner bell. There was never any of the abominable shilly-shallying so prevalent in the outside world, where, too often, the announcement of dinner is a signal for people to rush off to the bathroom or settle back to see the end of a TV program while the food quietly deteriorates on the table. At the Ticoma you could cook popovers and when they were done, strike the triangle, serenely confident that by the time you could lift the popovers from the oven sixty loggers would be at their places, waiting for them.

"Camp Push is sure giving you the once over," Meatball said, chuckling. He pointed out a big, shy-looking man sitting next to Old Fox at a table with a group of the bosses. Camp Push, he said, was boss on the job, second in command after Old Fox, the superintendent, who did not spend all his time at the camp by any means. Beside Camp Push sat the Bull Buck, headman in charge of fallers and buckers. "Why don't you go after the platters, Lee?" Meatball said. "They're all panting to get a closer look at you."

I wanted to mention that most of them already had seen an unprecedented proportion of me. But anyway, I knew I would have to get used to running the gauntlet so I straightened my skirts, held my chin up and stepped into the dining room.

Old Fox gave me a reassuring wink as I picked up the empty dishes during another resounding silence. This time the silence did not seem appalled. I even had a feeling it was rather an approving silence. Then all at once my morale soared. There was not a single biscuit left on a single table. I sashayed out of the dining room feeling like a prima donna who has just received a thundering ovation.

After the whipped-cream cake and strawberries were gone, a few of the men lit cigarettes with their coffee. Most of them just leaped up and tore out as if they were pursued. There were only four poker games going at the moment, Meatball explained, and all of them wanted to sit in.

Yet, in spite of their rush, each man picked up his own plate, stopped with it at a double-decker cart near the door, scraped it into a hole in the cart which had a pail under it, dropped the silverware down another hole into a dishpan full of hot, sudsy water, stacked his plate and mug and left.

I saw Camp Push motion to one man who left the table empty handed and as he returned sheepishly for his plate, the Bull Buck said, "Olaf wants to help with the dishes tonight. Can't say I blame him." Helping with the dishes I gathered was a penalty for leaving a plate on the table.

As soon as we had finished our own supper we cleaned up and reset the tables with thick white plates upside down at each place, coffee mugs turned over on the plates and white flour sacks covering the setups in the middle of the tables—the salt, pepper, sugar, catsup, steak sauce, tabasco sauce, jam or jelly, cans of extra teaspoons and holders of paper napkins. By that time coffee hounds had begun to drift in for another cup. I recognized Snoozy, the bull cook, still with a wad of snoose under his lip. Meatball introduced the others, Powder Box Pete, Indian Johnny, Moonshine Jake and a dozen or so more whose names all got mixed up in my mind.

The room was full of friendly kidding and fine deep laughter. Immediately I began to feel wonderfully popular. After living in a city where women are ten deep all over the place and even the streets smell of cosmetics, all the virility around me was wonderfully invigorating. Why, I discovered, I was little and fragile and absolutely *unique* in a man's world. Only I mustn't let it go to my head, I told myself, wishing Doug Weatherby could see me, surrounded by all those big, respectful, admiring men.

I noticed one unusually handsome young fellow who, Meatball said, was Mike Torbin, a cat skinner. I gathered cat skinners were looked up to as the daredevils of the camp.

"All he wants in life is to be as good a cat skinner as Wild Bill." Meatball shook his head. "Fat chance. Wild Bill's the greatest cat skinner in the state. He's away for a few days."

Oh my gosh, I thought, remembering a quick glint of eyes which had reminded me of a fractious horse. That was Wild Bill on the zoo bench. I had not thought of it before, but those two loggers were going to come right back here to Ticoma and they were going to be vastly surprised to see me already established. If they recognized me at all. I glanced up at Meatball, wondering if I should say, casually, "Oh yes, I think I've seen Wild Bill."

Meatball was not looking at me. His head was tipped in a listening attitude and then I too heard the car as it whined to a stop at the door. Of one accord all the men slowly put down their coffee cups, as if they knew quick footsteps on the porch of the cookhouse at night could only mean an emergency.

The man who rushed in was dripping wet and white faced. "Got any lanterns or flashlights?" he gasped. "A kid's missing. They were all playing on a raft—"

The men seemed to move as one body. The words were hardly out before they surged to the door. When I ran outside right behind them, I heard Meatball say, "There's lanterns in the sheethouse. Where's Swivelneck? He's got the keys."

"Got a dang good notion to find me some whistle cord," Moonshine Jake was saying. "We can rig up a light."

"There's a thousand feet of whistle cord in the filing shack, Jake," someone shouted. "I'll get the Louse. It has a new battery. You there, Snoozy, take the headlight bulbs out of that truck there."

Snoozy ran past me toward a truck and Mike Torbin yelled, "You, girl! Go beat hell out of that bell and rout those bums out."

I ran back to the porch and beat frantically and discordantly on the triangle. Men poured from the cabins, some still holding their poker hands. "Those loggers camped below the dam have lost a kid. Maybe in the river," Mike shouted.

Men piled into the nearest cars and roared across the bridge.

"Here," John Paul said, shoving two gas lanterns at me. "You hold these and get in front. Look out you don't kick the lantern pump out." I scrambled into his car and we shot across the bridge through choking dust that had a greasy taste to it from the cars ahead.

It was black at the dam, one of those moonless nights when not even the silhouettes of the trees could be seen. Only a few dim lights outlined the tents of the campers across the river. John Paul parked among the jammed cars and we climbed out. Above the thunder of the dam's waterfall from up on the hill we could hear a man's voice calling, "Jimmy! Jimmy!"

"Must be the kid's father," John Paul said, pumping up the gas lantern as I steadied it for him in the glow of the car's headlights. "Here, you guys make a windbreak," he called. "A breeze could break a mantel."

When the white light of the lanterns stabbed the darkness, John Paul carried them over to a group around a high-wheeled tough little crummy they called the Louse. Someone was holding a flashlight while Old Fox rigged the whistle cord to the Louse's battery.

"You girl," Old Fox said, "you hold the lantern for the boys while we get this blasted thing rigged. A man here said the kids were all fooling around on a raft below the dam. They didn't miss the little fellow until they all sat down to supper."

John Paul handed me a lantern and started to wade across the pool with the other. His light showed a group of women huddled on the riverbank. One glance at the little group was all I could bear and yet, even with that one glance, I knew in my heart that a tall, dark-haired girl standing close to the water was the child's mother.

I took a firmer grip on the lantern, forcing myself to remember what my father used to tell me when I was holding a light for him. "Hold it so you can see. Then I can see, too." So I held the light high enough to see the dark pool where the children had been playing.

A cordon of men had joined hands and waded out into the shoulder-deep pool and were sweeping the water with their feet, making pass after pass across it. When that proved of no use, they tore viciously at the high pile of driftwood lodged in the shallower water at the bottom of the pool, dislodging an empty oil drum that bounced as it hit the banks; the tangled roots of a huge stump, like a great animal in the night; a deadhead that took six men to move; then a limp mass that stopped my heart for a moment before I saw it was just a strip of bark.

I will never get that scene out of my mind, the lighted shapes of the men sifting through the debris, lifting logs that were unliftable and tossing them savagely to the bank, their grunts of effort drowned out by the dam's thunder, while above it all, on the hillside, the wild cry, "Jimmy! Jimmy!" knifed through the dark.

When the pile was demolished, we moved downstream to the next pool, lying silent, surrounded by huge rocks. Methodically, the men began to sweep this pool as they had the other. By that time the light was rigged below the dam. A glowing ball crawled on the river's bottom, haloed with a yellow mist, eerily crossing the water, back and forth, bank to bank. I could feel my breathing stop each time it lighted up a rock, a sunken can, another rock.

"It's no goddamn use. It's too damn late," I heard a huge logger mumble brokenly. The same thought must have been in everybody's mind, although it only seemed to make them redouble their efforts.

The ominous shriek of the falls grew louder as we moved downstream to the last jam of limbs and bark. I held the lantern as high as I could, only half aware that my arm had grown numb.

"Hold that lantern higher!" a rough voice yelled. Then, "Higher, dammit!"

I started to wade in, when a tall logger snatched the lantern from me and lifted it high. As the light struck the dam, a great shout rose that was cut off in mid-breath. I could see a little red head down there, among the tangle of limbs where the child was caught in the brush.

But his head is out of water, I thought, beginning to tremble. Those limbs held his head out—oh, thank God.

Half a dozen men had reached the jam. Gently they lifted the little boy from the tangled mess and above the noise of the falls I heard a faint whimper. Then I saw the child move.

There was not a single sound as Indian Johnny crossed

the swinging bridge toward the group of women, with the little boy in his arms. The men stood dripping and motionless. At that moment any sound would have been like yelling in church. Then they began moving silently toward the cars.

"Snoozy," Old Fox said, "you better go help the women warm him up fast. Hot-water bottles and hot blankets. Maybe a little hot toddy."

From the hillside we could still hear the desperate cry, "Jimmy!" The Bull Buck and Jake turned and raced up the slope toward the father and the rest of us stood there, shivering, until the father's flashlight turned down the mountain and he came crashing through the brush.

Someone gathered up the whistle cord and disconnected the battery. When we turned out the lantern it was pitch black again until the car lights began going on, one after the other, and we all went roaring back along the road to camp.

I crawled into my rib-gouging cot as tired and happy as I had ever been in my life. When I closed my eyes, I could see Indian Johnny again, crossing the bridge with the child in his arms. But mixed up with the bliss, I was conscious of another feeling. I kept remembering that cat skinner saying, "Girl, beat hell out of that bell," and Old Fox saying, "You, girl, hold the lantern for the boys." Just as I dropped asleep I knew what the feeling was. I felt necessary for the first time in several years.

chapter three

🍂 ACCORDING to the legend, when Paul Bunyan was logging in Oregon one winter the cookstove in camp covered a whole acre of ground. The flunkeys used to tie the side of a hog to each foot and skate around on the griddle to grease it, while the cook flipped the pancakes.

This story, I am convinced, was not made up at all. It came straight out of a nightmare disturbing the sleep of some harassed second cook. I have had dreams of the type myself, after frying hot cakes for sixty loggers.

Sixty loggers eat three hundred hot cakes every morning between six thirty and six forty-five. Of course they eat other things at the same time, meat for example (either bacon, ham or sausages), two hundred eggs and one hundred pieces of toast with jam or jelly, as well as coffee and mounds of hashed brown potatoes.

Days at the Ticoma logging camp always began the same way. I would drag myself out of bed at four in the morning, stagger to the sink and slosh cold water over my face until I came awake, hurry into my clothes and then set out toward the lights of the cookhouse, walking softly, so as not to waken the sleeping camp. I have never known anything as hushed as those dawns, with the evening's dust stilled and the hot sun still hidden. There was never so much as the cheep of a bird up in those Oregon woods. Just a vast silence.

40

Not that I had much time to grow philosophical about nature. Once in the cookhouse there would only be time to scramble into an apron and gulp down a cup of coffee before we would all be plunged into the most violent activity. First bell was at five thirty to wake up the men; second at six, when the men started loading their lunch buckets; breakfast at six thirty.

The first time I saw the lunch counter set up, it looked to me like an agricultural display representing America's Plenty. It stretched, forty feet long and five feet wide, down the middle of a lunchroom adjoining the kitchen. The table was completely hidden by the food on it: bread, butter, lettuce, sliced raw onions, rings of green peppers, three kinds of cheese, roast pork and beef, slices of boiled ham, egg salad, tuna fish mix, bologna, liver sausage, thüringer, corned beef, spiced tongue and heart, pickles, olives (ripe and green stuffed), cakes, cookies, apple pies, berry pies, a basket of oranges and white enameled pitchers of milk.

"Great Scott!" I said to John Paul who was lugging in two huge bowls of canned peaches to add to the volume. "Haven't you forgotten something?"

"I hope not," John Paul said and looked worried. "You mean sardines? We only put those out on Fridays."

That first morning Meatball asked me if I could fry hot cakes. At the time we were loading baking pans with bacon, overlapping the strips in order to get the trayful into two pans.

"Well, I ought to be able to," I told him airily. "Shall I mix the batter?"

Meatball gave me a considering look, by which I gathered the making of hot cakes at Ticoma was a matter of considerable importance and any failure a serious offense.

Finally he seemed to nerve himself up to bold action and told me, yes I could prepare the batter and that I would find the amounts written on a tablet.

I started the job with confidence. Years before, my mother had taught me the secret of light, tender hot cakes, so I followed her directions and after all the other ingredients had been thoroughly beaten, in a five-gallon electric beater, I added the baking powder last, stirred it in by hand with a great gentleness and watched out of the corner of my eye as Meatball came over to inspect the results. He was magnanimous about the airiness of the dough. He even said it looked lighter than his batter.

At six o'clock sharp he beat second bell on the triangle; the men descended in hordes on the lunch table and in the kitchen we cleared our decks for action—toast being kept warm, hashbrowns lifted onto platters, coffee made for both breakfast table and thermos jugs, the six-foot grill dribbled over with oil and wiped with a pad of bleached gunny sacking. Finally Meatball and I took up our battle stations, Meatball frying the eggs and I the hot cakes.

Meatball was a portly man (plump as a dumpling in fact) and moved with dignity, but a ballet dancer could not have performed with greater precision, the quality, I suspect, which separates the real cooks from the tyros who go to pieces when everything is happening on the stove at the same moment. As for me, within two minutes I was coming apart at the seams.

First there was the batter to be poured out of a pitcher, in identical mounds and precise rows. I could get exactly forty-eight on the grill before the first one was ready to turn. Then the frantic flipping began, to keep up with all those dozens of golden cakes. Slide, flip, plop—and try to make each one land in the exact spot it came from. Slide, flip, plop—and if you once get behind you'll be totally lost with row after row growing black before you can catch up with them again.

Meatball and I ended neck and neck, egg platters full, hot cakes ready. As John Paul carried the last load into the dining room, I beat out an amateurish tune on the triangle and the men who had been clustered in famished groups near the lunch counter all came rushing to their places. I do not believe they came actually roaring with hunger. That was simply an impression I had. The lunch counter, I saw to my astonishment, was denuded, although I had only time to glance at it. Meatball and I were back at the stove frying like mad to keep up with the refills.

By the time the men pushed their plates back, I felt as if I had run a country mile. Meatball, on the other hand, looked as composed as ever when the men left and we settled down for our own breakfast at a table which John Paul had wiped clean. For a few minutes I just sat there, trying to catch my breath.

The bedlam of the logging crew's departure still seemed to hang in the morning air, like the blue puffs of diesel and gasoline which hovered above the powdered dust of the yard. Long after they had gone, it rang in my ears— the revving of motors on the huge, red logging trucks and the rattling of their bunkers; the clatter of the ponderous yellow Caterpillars; the clang of gear being loaded onto trucks, the cable, tongs, axes, wedges and chain saws; the tinny jangle of lunch buckets jostling one another under the plank seats of the crummies; the shouts of the men and the tramp of calk boots on the splintered walk.

"Loggers are lonely men," Meatball said with the air of a sage, comfortably helping himself to seven hot cakes and a quarter pound of butter. "There's a history behind most of them except the young kids. Broken lives, wives dead or divorced. Some of them are hiding out so they won't have to pay alimony. We've even got two or three who are on parole from the penitentiary.

"And a good many," he went on, "just never could get along anywhere but in a logging camp."

I told him they looked happy enough to me. Better adjusted than city men, more relaxed and confident.

"Happy?" he snorted. "What's 'happy?' Sure, they're happy enough in a way. A good place to eat and a bed. The camp's even a sort of family."

At the moment I was feeling awed by loggers. Memories of the night before and their titanic labors by the dam were still fresh in my mind. I thought I liked them all. That was before I met Swivelneck.

Swivelneck ran the commissary, which stocked a variety of manly wares, from T-shirts, shorts, jeans, blue calico shirts, rain clothes and calk boots to razors, playing cards, pipes and round boxes of Copenhagen snuff, practically everything a logger needs except whiskey and women. It might have had the pleasant atmosphere of a country store if it had not been for Swivelneck.

I ran afoul of him shortly after breakfast. At that time I was supposed to make pies for the next day's lunch table. Ordinarily, I would also have cakes or cookies to bake, but since I was new to the job, Meatball said he would take over that chore for the day and that I could confine myself to baking pies. Twenty of them. Ten apple pies, five pumpkin pies and five rhubarb pies. The very thought made my heart slide down to my toes.

I had the cookhouse to myself for the stint. John Paul had washed up and left and Meatball was off somewhere, probably with his paperback love story. Now it is one thing to make a pie or two with loving care and present it to an admiring family and quite another thing to turn them out by the dozen. I set to work, rather nervously, at the pie board, measuring out flour according to the specifications on the tablet and working it into the shortening. The job went slowly, but little by little the aroma of apple pies baking in the ovens drove out the hot stifling smell of dust and diesel. The only sound in camp was the humming of a chain saw across the river. I began to feel pressed. Already pie dough was sticking to my fingers. It was going to be another muggy day.

The buzzing of the saw had stopped, I noticed, and then, suddenly, off in the distance, I heard the cry *timber!* and forgot heat and pies in a second. I did not even wipe the pie dough from my hands. I just ran out to watch from the back porch of the cookhouse. For an instant there was the renewed whirr of the chain saw and after that stillness.

With something like a sigh, a huge fir on the hill across from me began its majestic descent. It fell slowly and sedately, its great green arms outstretched. Then halfway down something went wrong. Some vagrant wind or a weakness in the sinew of the mammoth fir made it snap in mid-air and crash ignominiously to the foot of the mountain.

As the booming echo faded on the opposite hill, I turned to go back to my pies, and instead stopped dead in my tracks, hardly believing what I saw. Another magnificent tree slid ponderously against the stump of the fallen fir, holding its own pallet of moss and tangled underbrush in its clutching roots. It hesitated there, weaving precariously like a tightrope walker who has lost his balance, until, with a final defeated dance, it toppled to join the tree below. Then slowly the whole mountainside went mad. Tree after tree crashed over. They came down in wild confusion, breaking and splintering into a worthless jumble in the river far below.

Above them a strip of bare rock, perhaps a hundred and twenty-five-feet wide, reached to the hilltop, a naked gash of crumbling shale where a few moments before there had been a lovely wooded slope. A huge mass of debris, of splintered trees and jagged rock, twisted brush and powdered shale jutted halfway across the little river.

The only person I could see in camp was Swivelneck watching from the door of the commissary. "The men!" I screamed at him. "Are they all right?"

He just stood there, so I jumped off the porch and rushed over to his door. "What happened to the men who cut down that tree?"

Swivelneck looked me over slowly, the dough on my hands, the flour in my hair. "You don't cut down trees," he said, looking disgusted. "You 'fell' them. Though some of these guys say 'fall.' If they hear you say 'cut,' you'll be laughed out of camp."

"But the men!" I shouted. "Were they hurt?"

"Of course not," he said. "Did you think they just stood at the base of the tree? Old Fox has been warning them about that ground for days." He pointed a long finger toward the edge of the slide and I could make out two men picking up their saw and gear.

"I see they saved their saw, too," Swivelneck went on. "It's nothing to those bums that Coos Pacific has just lost a hundred thousand feet of timber." He was a thin, pale man with a glandular look and prominent ears.

I let out my breath in relief. "Thank heaven the fallers are safe."

Swivelneck laughed. "You can always find more men but timber is getting prettty scarce."

46

A macabre joke and it did not strike me as funny. I frowned at him in outrage. The outrage was entirely lost on Swivelneck. He was not noticing my face anyway. Instead he surveyed the terrain from my neck down, apparently with quickened interest, because all at once he looked waggish. He walked down the steps and stood beside me, taking on an air of masculine dominance. Then the jackass, with a silly grin on his face, reached out and gave me a pinch.

There are ways of discouraging pinches without unduly antagonizing the pincher. But what I did was jump like a goosed gazelle and cry out, "Keep your dirty hands off me!"

I think, subconsciously, I expected to have to fight for my virtue, alone up there with sixty virile loggers, and therefore automatically showed my teeth at the first wolf cry.

Swivelneck's grin congealed on his face. Well, I've made an enemy, I thought, trudging back toward the cookhouse. It was even possible the man could have me fired. Then I remembered the pies in the oven and broke into a dead run.

Luckily the burning smell which greeted me as I burst into the cookhouse came not from pies but from some of the apple boiling over into the oven. The pies themselves were safe. But it was already nine fifteen and by that time the remainder of the dough was too sticky to be workable. If I added flour I was afraid the crust would be tough, so I carried the dough into the walk-in and while it chilled, began recklessly throwing salt, sugar, spices, eggs and milk into some canned pumpkin, all the time a prey to terrified thoughts. Although Meatball had written down the weights of flour and shortening for twenty pies (a far larger proportion of shortening than I had ever used before), he had not specified the amounts of salt and water. I had had to guess. Moreover the ovens were untried strangers to me. I kept remembering occasions when something had gone wrong with my pies and I had been obliged to dip them up with a spoon. If such a thing happened today, I thought hysterically, I shall throw myself into the Ticoma.

Well, anyway, twenty pies were baked and ranged on the pieboard by the time Meatball arrived at eleven. True, some of the apple had burst their seams and the pumpkin had slightly scorched edges. But then I felt a little singed myself. Tactfully Meatball ignored the confusion in the kitchen, the flour all over the floor and me, my face, beet red with heat and exertion, and my hands trembling with nervousness. He even smiled at me benignly and suggested that I have a glass of cold fruit juice. He had a new paperback with him, I noticed. Another love story. Somewhat reluctantly, he put it aside to instruct me in camp life.

First he gave me the scuttlebutt on Swivelneck. I did not tell him the cause of our hostility, just that our meeting was not very friendly. "Don't pay any attention to the bastard," he said. The man who usually ran the commissary, both well and efficiently—a fellow named Harry—was away on leave, he told me, so Swivelneck had been hired to fill in. In the opinion of the loggers, he was gumshoeing around, hoping to ingratiate himself with the company by turning up a lot of waste. "Well," he said, "if he comes around here anymore with his beefs about why don't we use those old stale crackers instead of buying more, I'll take after him with a cleaver. And so help me, I'll catch up with him, too. He's a perfect example of a company man."

I stared at him, perfectly fascinated. With his eyebrows pulled down that way he did not look like a fat, good-natured cook anymore. He looked like a baldheaded eagle. He shook his head lugubriously when I described the slide.

He had heard of such things, he said, but had never seen one himself.

Later in the day he instructed me further, this time on the eating habits of loggers. In a logging camp, I learned, you do not have to bother about what the bosses think of your food. It is the men you must keep a weather eye on.

During the bosses' noon meal, Meatball and John Paul had been leaning against the pieboard, watching the dozen and a half men in the dining room tying into their dinner, one which had been most ample and, in my way of thinking, excellent, too.

"I heard Camp Push say, 'What! Hash again!'" John Paul told Meatball in a low voice.

Meatball chuckled and turned an amused face toward me. "I feed the bosses leftovers at noon and maybe I have been overdoing the hash lately. Leftovers is a dirty word in a logging camp. What I can't palm off on the bosses goes into the garbage can. I wouldn't dare try to feed any to the men."

If the men become annoyed with a cook, he said, they would call a meeting. Dread of a loggers' meeting hung continuously over the heads of the kitchen crew. Not that the loggers would come storming out and lynch the cook or even tar and feather him. Cooks did not wait to find out what *would* happen. At the first rumble of discontent or rumor that a meeting was about to be called, the cook would take off down the road with all his gear as if the devil were after him.

A camp was rated primarily by the quality of the food served. It went without saying that quantity was always there. Nothing disgraced a cook so fast as to run out of something. The only comparable offense was to serve lamb. Loggers refused to be fed lamb. It had to be turkey or chicken once a week, steak on Wednesday nights, baked ham, roast pork, roast beef or roast veal in between times, hamburger once or twice a month and fish every Friday, in addition to a minor entree such as liver and onions or macaroni and cheese.

On steak nights, the cook could slip them less popular vegetables, spinach, turnips, beets or asparagus, to vary the diet from their favorites, their favorites being potatoes, any kind of dried beans, corn, peas, tomatoes and creamed string beans in that order. Hot bread must be served every night and for dessert, since loggers ate so much pie at noon, they expected either pudding, ice cream and cake, or strawberries, fresh or frozen.

That afternoon, as I settled down for my nap, I reviewed the situation. My pies had passed muster with Meatball; the loggers had liked my biscuits and hot cakes. The worst of my initiation, I thought, was over. I had been put to the test and had not been found wanting. And then the eggs hit the electric fan.

It happened that night at supper, without warning. I hurried into the dining room with a platter full of fried chicken and there were the two boys from Fleishacker Zoo, Wild Bill and Ed, settled at a table, being jovially hailed by loggers at the neighboring tables. At my first glance I could see that these were notable personalities in camp. Particularly Wild Bill. He was even more dramatic than I remembered, tall, with a steel-springed look about him and a daredevil air. The younger cat skinners seemed to follow his every move with a sort of awe.

Well, the boys are in for a little surprise, that's all, I told myself and avoided glancing in Wild Bill's direction a second time. Instead I stooped over to pick up a gravy bowl and found myself looking directly into Ed's remarkably candid blue eyes. For a moment I saw a startled recognition in them. What he saw in mine must have been apprehension because, to my relief, he glanced quickly away and down at his plate. But as I started toward the door, Wild Bill exclaimed, "Say, Ed, ain't that the gal we saw in the zoo?"

"Shut up, you dope. She'll hear you," Ed said.

"It sure as hell is," Wild Bill went on, lowering his voice only a little. "That's the doll was sitting on the bench in San Francisco listening at us near monkey island."

There was a short, amazed silence at the table, and then a whoop of laughter which sounded to me like an explosion. "Vell," I heard Hans roar out, "I ain't seen a skirt yet as von't folla Vild Beel furder den dat."

And there, I realized with a shock, was the story which the whole camp was going to believe. By morning I would be known as the girl who had followed Wild Bill all the way up from San Francisco after getting just one look at him.

Thinking it over afterward I realized that if any logger except Wild Bill had been sitting on that bench at the zoo—Powder Box Pete, for example, or Moonshine Jake—nobody would have given the matter a second thought. It was Wild Bill's reputation that made the affair sensational. The loggers expected drama wherever he went.

Possibly every logging camp has some such personage. In the old ripsnorting days it would have been the man who could drink more, spit further, roar louder and fight harder than any other "timber beast" in the vicinity. Wild Bill's reputation did not hang on any such outrageous talents. He was just, in the opinion of the camp, the best damn cat skinner in the world. He could balance one track over a cliff, so they said, with the other in the sky. He had even been known to whirl his Cat around in a lightning maneuver, lift its blade as if it were a catcher's mitt and fend off a runaway log, hurtling down on a group of loggers in the canyon below. As a secondary characteristic, he had a store of ribald yarns which would have made the old Whiz Bang read like a sermon and a reputation for success with women bordering on the fabulous.

All this I learned later. At the time I just felt stunned. My only coherent thought had to do with the possible reaction of Old Fox, who had warned me so sternly against "monkey shines." Old Fox was not in camp that night. But he was bound to hear the story. I had caught a glimpse of Swivelneck half turned in his chair, his over-sized ears practically flapping.

During my childhood my father had instructed me to climb right back onto a horse if it threw me and if any job seemed impossible, to tackle it immediately. Automatically I turned around and marched back into the dining room to gather up all the biscuit platters with a do-your-damndest attitude. Whether the hilarity in there was still at my expense I do not know. I was too busy stalking from table to table, trying to keep my dignity.

After supper I raced through the evening's work, determined to be well away from the cookhouse before the coffee hounds began drifting back with more heavy-handed humor. It was not my lucky evening. I heard voices in the kitchen while I was still slicing onions for the next day's lunch table. They were mild Bermuda onions. Even so tears were blurring my eyes when I looked up and saw Ed standing watching me. The sight of my damp eyes seemed to increase his obvious discomfiture.

"Look, I wanted to explain," he began.

"What's there to explain?" I demanded, hacking furiously at an onion and barely missing my thumb.

"Well, it's about Wild Bill. That's the best guy in camp."

I gave something like a snort.

"He wouldn't deliberately hurt a mouse," Ed said. "He really didn't mean any harm and he wasn't bragging, either. He doesn't have to. All the girls just naturally go for him."

"For Pete's sake," I cried out. "You agree with all those laughing hyenas out there—"

Ed shoved his hands into his pockets and seemed to stand a little taller. "Don't let anybody hear you talking about the loggers like that or you're a dead duck up here."

I wanted to tell him that I was already a dead duck, thanks to his friend Wild Bill. A glance at his face silenced me. It was a good, rugged face, sun and wind tanned, and his concern seemed real, so instead I muttered, "Thanks. I'll remember."

He kept on watching me while I wrapped aluminum foil around the onions and took them into the walk-in. When I came out he was still there. He followed me out of the back door, keeping pace with me all the way to the Old Homestead. "Look," he said, stopping at the foot of the rickety steps. "These guys are always razzing somebody. They'll forget about it in a few days. So don't lose any sleep over it." He made a vague gesture which might have been taken for an encouraging salute and walked off.

I slumped onto the chopping-block seat on my porch. The heat had begun to leave the valley and the dust had settled down. Some of the bunkhouses showed a pale glow from their windows but only the bosses' cabin, with a poker game in progress, was brightly lighted. Now and then I heard an exclamation or a burst of laughter from there. Otherwise the camp was quiet, except for the murmur of the nearby riffle and a contented grunting coming up through the floor boards, where the old sow and her brood were settling down for the night.

I never wanted the sun to rise again. I did not want to face a new day and sixty grinning loggers. I did not want to make hot cakes for them. Or biscuits. Or pies. Another woman up here with all these men, I thought, would have had them eating out of her hand. But not me. Within thirty-six hours, I turn out to be an object of ridicule, a laughing stock, a figure of fun.

The irony of it particularly outraged me. Here I was accused of chasing after Wild Bill when, in actual fact, I had been running away from thoughts of quite a different man, one of far greater magnetism than any crazy cat skinner who ever lived, I told myself.

Swivelneck lost no time spreading the word about. I was having midmorning coffee with Meatball and John Paul when the door of the cookhouse was thrown open with unusual force. I had heard the pickup outside and looked up, expecting to see Old Fox walk in. Instead a woman was standing on the threshold. A big, robust woman. She filled the entire doorway.

"I thought you said you keep 'em busy," she said over her shoulder.

"They usually are," a meek voice replied behind her.

The woman surged on into the kitchen with our boss following along after her, very much the tail of a kite. Meatball and John Paul jumped up.

"Can I get you some coffee, Mrs. Knowland?" John Paul asked, reaching for the coffee mugs.

"Yes, siree. I could do with some pie, too. I'm starved, getting up at the crack of dawn."

"At eight o'clock, she means," Old Fox put in.

54

"As I was saying, at the crack of dawn. And then jiggling all the way up here in that pickup. Every bone in the body is tore loose."

For the first time in camp I saw the movie version of a logger's costume. Mrs. Knowland was wearing a bright plaid shirt and smooth hiking pants. They looked as if they were encasing a couple of oil drums. The pants were made of sturdy stuff, but when she stepped over the bench and sat down, I could almost hear the seams pop. The bench was only a third wide enough for her. She might have been sitting on a rail.

I stole a glance at the boss. Old Fox had not shrunk an inch. He was as vital as ever, and he was looking at his wife with evident pride. But even a war horse, snorting and pawing the earth, would have seemed tame compared to Mrs. Knowland.

"Lee, meet the wife," he said. When he glanced at me, I noticed, his face became a little grave.

She nodded graciously enough, but with a measuring glance which I found disconcerting. "Well," she said, "you boys run along now. This girl and I have some talking to do." She motioned toward the door with her flamboyantly blond head.

It's not going to be any cozy womanly chat, either, I thought, as the three men filed out.

"I hear you come from San Francisco," she began. I nodded and her face took on a disapproving expression, as if the admission, in her mind, placed me right away among the call girls.

"What'd you do there for a living?" she asked, narrowing her quite fine brown eyes suspiciously.

"I worked some for a cateress," I told her. It sounded pretty lame.

"It's quite a little distance to San Francisco. How come you hightailed it all the way up here to the Ticoma for a job?"

"Well, I happened to overhear two loggers saying there was a second cook's job open," I began.

"So I hear," Mrs. Knowland interrupted. "And one of them just happened to be Wild Bill Moran." She brought one hand, a surprisingly delicate and girlish hand, down on the table with a bang. "Well," she said, "we're not going to have any trouble in *this* camp. Wild Bill is—"

"I don't give a damn about Wild Bill," I cried out. Being so keyed up, I said a great deal more than I intended to. I told her exactly how I had felt after losing my one chance at a good job, and of the way the words "Coos Bay" had sung in my soul.

"Well, can you beat that!" Mrs. Knowland exclaimed, when I ran down a little. "So you were brought up on the lower river." This seemed to make a great deal of difference to her. She leaned back, studying me, as if she were trying to adjust her mind to a new concept. "Brought up on the lower river," she repeated. "Why, so was I." She looked quite benevolent and protective all at once. "You did right, girl, coming back here. California's no place for an Oregonian. And don't let's have any more talk about being a failure. You'll get along just fine. Casper told me you were doing a good job."

Casper, I supposed, was Old Fox.

She fell to eating her pie with relish. "Don't mind my jumping on you, the way I did," she said apologetically. "You wouldn't have been the first girl to follow Wild Bill up here. And the men don't get much work done when they're brawling over some tramp.

"Though I might have known you weren't that type,"

she added hurriedly. "Casper's been telling me how you're always bustling about. He says it reminds him of the way I used to flip my tail around the cookhouse."

I believe she started talking to soothe me, because she could see I was wrought up. She said logging camps were nothing new to her. She had been running a cookhouse before I was even thought of. "I didn't weigh as much as you, in those days, either, and my hair hung down to my waist, just the color of a Jersey cow." Pretty soon, I think she forgot all about me and was right back in the tough old days—days, I believe, which had grown more rugged year by year in her memory. Loggers then were all splendid young bucks, not at all like the crowbait we had in camp now, according to Mrs. Knowland.

Their feats with the ax were legendary and their fights absolutely shook the earth. They weren't softies, either, demanding their bacon and choice ham and sausages. They'd light into side pork and fried corn-meal mush and the beans she always kept cooking in the big kettles. The cracks in the bunkhouses were so wide they never needed windows and the board bunks were stacked three high— that's what caused a lot of fights, a man waking up to find some joker's calk boot in his face.

On Saturday nights, when they'd pile into the launch and sing all the way to Marshfield, the town really knew they were coming. "We'd sound like a herd of cattle clattering along the wooden sidewalk. And when we'd come into the dance hall, boy! How they'd cheer. The girls, sitting around the dance floor in their high-topped shoes, would perk up like fresh-watered cabbage. I'd never dance more than a couple of minutes with any one fellow before somebody else cut in. I could have had my pick of the camp. Forty men there were, too. I picked Casper."

"You chose well," I put in.

"You bet I did. I liked him the moment I clapped eyes on him.

"He was a cocky little runt even then," she added affectionately. Then she planted her hands on her thighs and heaved herself to her feet. "Now back you go to your cabin, Lee. I'll bake the pies today."

"Oh no, Mrs. Knowland," I protested.

"Just call me Hortense. And off you go," she said, in a tone of voice which told me she expected people to hop to it when she gave an order. As I started out of the cookhouse, I heard her calling out to Old Fox: "I'm doing the baking today. That poor kid is about tuckered out. You can stay and talk to me."

"But baby, I should be out in the woods!"

"Rot! You look pukey. What are you trying to do, work yourself up to a wingding?"

"Now baby—"

"Don't you 'now baby' me," she mimicked. "I haven't lived with you for thirty years for nothing. I can spot a binge coming on a mile away."

Hortense, I believe, was the world's best pie maker. When I got back to the cookhouse, after the ineffable luxury of a morning nap, Hortense's blond head was tousled, her gay red face was dotted with flour, and lined up on the pieboard were rows of flaky pies and fancy, decorated cookies. I have never seen such golden, tender pie crust. Hortense said it was easy. She said she used the same measurements of flour and shortening as we had written on the tablet. The measurements had originally come from her. Sixteen ounces of flour to eleven of shortening. Then, she said, she put in enough salt to make the flour taste of it a little, and worked it very thoroughly until there was not a speck of uncoated flour. She said she never used anything but a two-tined fork to mix the ice water in with and she wasn't stingy with the water, either. "Add water till the dough feels like you had a baby's cheek in your hands. Then you can handle the dough as much as you like and no damage done."

Pie making was not the only good job Hortense did that day. She also passed around a corrected version of the zoo bench incident. I believe the story Hortense relayed to the camp had been worked on a bit by her powerful imagination, too. In it, I imagine, the poor girl who had fled back to her old home from the heartless city had been not only unemployed, but probably hungry and homeless as well.

The results were quite apparent in the loggers' attitude at supper that night. Loggers are pushovers for a sad story. There was not the slightest reference to Wild Bill. Instead I was conscious of an added consideration. There were even some friendly remarks passed about the excellence of the corn bread I had made.

Wild Bill himself seemed to be the only person who was not convinced. He kept his eyes strictly to the front, except once when he thought nobody was looking. Then he grinned at me out of the side of his mouth and slowly lowered his left eyelid.

chapter four

ONE morning at breakfast I overheard Camp Push saying, "Jake, you get rid of that old bitch today. I think she's a conky old bitch and these still days give me the willies."

This cryptic remark meant absolutely nothing to me. Everything in camp had some curious name. Crews were "sides"; a donkey was a huge piece of machinery with drums to reel in the cable and an efficient way of bellying up steep mountains; a tin ass was a small cable and a skidder was an unusually big donkey. A bull-prick was a rod or powder bar used in dynamiting, but the Bull Buck was the boss in charge of the cutting crew, of the fallers, who felled the trees, and the buckers who limbed them and cut them into log lengths.

As far as I was concerned, a "conky old bitch" could have been anything from a disagreeable elderly woman to a machine for making doughnuts. I thought no more about the remark until afternoon, when I was in the shower.

Up to that time I had done my bathing in the river but, in accordance with orders posted by Old Fox, the bath house was now mine every day between two and three. This sounded luxurious, until I saw the bath house. It was built of perpendicular planks, the cracks giving it a breezy, open-air effect and letting in the sunlight in shimmering little rays. It looked to me like a Peeping Tom's delight.

The place had two shower stalls and a square, kitchen type of sink. Since the floor was splintery and I suspected it of harboring athlete's foot, I kept on my slippers and tossed my towel and bathrobe over two spikes high up on the wall. I had just stepped under the shower of spring water, as soft as kitten fur, when I heard the rattly-bang of arriving crummies and realized with annoyance that the men were coming in early. Since they all would want showers, I felt I had to leave promptly.

Outside the clamor died down to a murmur and above the murmur a chain saw whirred monotonously. As I reached for my robe, somebody yelled *timber!* It sounded practically in my ear. Oh my gosh, I thought. The conky old bitch! Camp Push had been talking about a *tree,* and Jake was felling it.

Pulling frantically at my robe I heard a yell, "Everybody out of camp! Run, you bums! It's leaning this way."

I pulled desperately. The robe was caught fast on the spike, out of my reach. Even when I jumped as high as I could, it still would not budge. I could not tear it off, either, although I jerked with all my strength.

"Run!" a voice shouted again as the chain saw quickened for its final sizz.

Feeling like some kind of a trapped animal, I snatched up the towel and wrapped it around me. As I darted outside, heading toward my cabin, someone yelled, "The other way!"

I looked up. The tree seemed to be towering directly over me. To my terrified eyes, it looked alive, an ogre looming above my head, dancing, waving its arms to cover the whole sky. I turned to run toward the hill in back of the bunkhouses, where a group of loggers had taken refuge, and as I ran, the valley shook with the impact of the fall.

There was a startled silence, followed by relieved laughter. Instead of hitting camp, the tree had turned to fall lengthwise in the river. In the general confusion, I tried to sneak away, unobserved. A trickle of amused laughter followed me, but it was sympathetic laughter. Thanks to Hortense's story, the camp had accepted me wholeheartedly as a "lady" and being a lady, in the opinion of the camp, I was not to be treated irreverently.

Now this was all very well and good, but living up to a logger's idea of a lady was an exacting business I discovered very soon. No hijinks at all. Not even a good hearty "damn" now and then. If you were a lady, you could not use any expression stronger than "oh dear," except under the strongest provocation. Nor could you wear pants or tight-fitting sweaters around the cookhouse. Even uniforms were out. Not feminine enough. You wore starchy cotton dresses, preferably of rose pink, daffodil yellow or cornflower blue. You never went anywhere near the bunkhouses unless a logger was gravely sick and your ministrations were needed. You could not even go near the loggers' work, during a weekday, except by special arrangement and accompanied by one of the bosses, although on Sunday it was proper to go out and exclaim in wonder at the magnificent job they were doing, if a logger invited and accompanied you.

Above all you did not make trouble. "Making trouble" was the worst thing a woman could do and consisted mainly of starting loggers to fighting, which they had a tendency to do anyway, like mountain elk during the rutting season. A woman was frowned sternly upon if she had more than one logger on the string at a time or played one off against another. Instead, you were expected to smile impersonally on all of them and take care not to slip anyone an extra-large apple dumpling.

If you followed all these stringent rules, you found yourself basking in universal approval. Within a week I began to wonder why I had never before realized how utterly bewitching I was. It creeps up on you, this sort of thing, coffee hounds in the evening vying for a word with you, the eyes of the older loggers softening with memories when they look at you, young bucks showing a tendency to swagger a bit if you glanced their way. I kept reminding myself that Gertie the sow and I were the only female creatures for miles around. It did no good. The only way I could get my feet on the ground and stop feeling like a composite of Queen Victoria and Helen of Troy was to stare hard at myself in the wavy mirror in the Old Homestead. That brought me back to earth every time.

My principal contact with individual loggers came during the evening coffee sessions, when most of the news and jokes of the camp washed through the cookhouse. There were certain personalities whose oddities were always being discussed.

Old Snoozy, the bull cook, for example, was chiefly famous for nipping away at anything with even a slight alcoholic content and then sleeping it off in the sheethouse afterward. At one time Snoozy had owned a prosperous contracting business in California. Whenever he had a good bun on, he would go around shaking his head and saying, "I drank up my job; I drank up my home and God damn if I didn't drink up my wife, too."

Yet little old Snoozy, with his bald head fringed by a few grey hairs in back, his "bumlago" and his perpetual wad of snoose shoving out his lower lip, was a man with a dream. If he felt you were his friend, he would pull out his bank book and point to the balance—over $2000 when he first showed it to me. His goal was $7000, with which he intended to buy a new car, a new wardrobe and some store teeth. He was then going to descend upon his family in Berkeley and make a splash. Whenever a logger mentioned Snoozy's big dream, however, it was with fingers crossed.

Every evening I heard some new guess about the location of a still which Moonshine Jake was rumored to have hidden somewhere in the woods, a rumor Jake never bothered to deny. Moonshine Jake never bothered to deny anything. He was the most ornery-looking man in camp, with a formidable jaw, white hair cropped close all over his head and a face and neck carved and furrowed by sixty years of violent living. Only a jaunty, four-toothed smile relieved the general cussedness of his appearance.

Although he weighed only about a hundred and twenty pounds with his calk boots on, out at the works he was a giant. He could chase Cat, fell or buck or boss a side and, if need arose, he was not above filling in as a choker setter, too—a man who sets tongs in the logs and is generally considered the lowest form of life in the woods.

Moonshine Jake had been a Wobbly—a member of the I.W.W.—back in the days when the Wobs were keeping the logging camps in a condition of the wildest uproar. I asked him once how the Wobblies got their name and he told me there were several versions, but he preferred the one about a Chinese restaurant man who had been engaged to feed members of the I.W.W. during a strike. Naturally every bum in the vicinity tried to cadge a free meal. The Chinaman would ask each one: "Are you I.W.W.?" But it sounded more like: "All loo eye wobble wobble?" For some reason the name stuck.

64

One evening, when Jake dropped in at the cookhouse between poker sessions, I asked him to sing us an old Wobbly song and to the tune of "The Wearing of the Green," in a roaring bass, he broke out with:

> There are wisely framed injunctions that you must not leave your job
> And a peaceable assemblage is declared to be a mob,
> And Congress passed a measure framed by some consummate ass,
> So they're clubbing men and women just for walking on the grass.

We all applauded loudly but Moonshine Jake gave us a wry glance. I think the song sounded exactly as dated to him as it did to us, for all it had inflamed hearts back around World War I. "And nowadays there's guys taking morning siestas all over the woods and thumbing their noses at the bosses," he said, shaking his head in a bewildered fashion. He turned on one of his likeable smiles. "Nobody has to wait for pie in the sky any more, do they, Lee? Not with you at the pieboard, they don't."

To my surprise, I learned that John Paul was also considered one of the camp characters. John Paul was always gravely pleasant, but he seldom opened his mouth and hardly seemed the type to embroil himself in a flamboyant situation. Yet he had become an object of great curiosity from the moment he arrived in camp, only two weeks before I did, driving up from Coos Bay with all his gear and with a large Coca-Cola ad strapped to the roof of the cab. This ad, the cutout of a girl, he had lugged carefully into his cabin and had firmly closed the door on her, while the loggers stood around and watched.

65

A man cannot do a thing like that in a logging camp without causing comment. Particularly since John Paul met all questions and kidding on the subject with his usual noncommittal expression.

I saw the Coca-Cola girl myself once. John Paul had offered to carry an extra mattress from his cabin to replace the pad on my cot, which by comparison would have made a Hindu fakir's bed of spikes feel downy. As I held open his cabin door while he wrestled the mattress out, I looked straight into his remarkably tidy room, blankets and sheets pulled taut on the cot, shoes in a precise row. The Coca-Cola ad stood against the wall at the foot of his bed and dominated the cabin. It was the usual ad, a pretty girl, life sized, smiling and holding up a bottle with the motto, "The Pause That Refreshes."

Well, I thought, if a man wants a Coca-Cola ad for a pinup girl, where's the harm? All the same, it seemed a little odd.

The affair seemed even odder a few days later when John Paul told me his story. At the time we were sitting on the cookhouse steps, peeling potatoes. Because of the heat John Paul had shed his shirt and was resplendent in all his tattoos. They reached only to his wrists. His hands I noticed were slender and fine, quite at variance with all the barbarity above them.

At first I tried to enliven our job with a little conversation. It fell absolutely flat. Finally I gave up and peeled away in silence. There was a hula girl on the man's stomach which wriggled slightly as he breathed and a grinning skull on his upper arm among the rose vines, which opened its jaw horribly when he tensed his biceps. These things kept me amused at first, although whenever I glanced at his face, I felt gloomy again. Those pale-blue eyes of his looked not only puzzled, but hurt, too.

He must have noticed my preoccupation with the art work which decorated him. All at once he laid down his knife and with one finger tapped the center of his chest where the four cupids held up a scroll with the name "Agnes" on it. "She haunts me," he said.

Naturally I assumed that Agnes haunted him in the way memories haunt all of us. But that was not what John Paul meant at all. To hear John Paul tell it, he was the object of a real, other-world haunting, and Agnes a ghostly presence which never left him. "She won't let up on me," he said.

You simply do not argue with a man as convinced as John Paul was. I sat there flabbergasted while with a melancholy dignity, he described the terrible situation he found himself in. He must have reached a point when, finally, he had to talk. Agnes, he said, had been his girl when he was a young buck first starting to sea. A pretty seamy character, too, I suspected, although John Paul did not say so. He said she was a little older than he, but a fine, strong girl, with a lot of life to her, who had lived in Seattle.

Through the years his memories of her had grown misty around the edges. The one thing which cut through all the intervening time and space was her laugh, a wild loud laugh like the voice of a sea bird.

During one trip, while he was in Singapore, he had had her name tattooed on his chest and showed it to her the next time his ship called in Seattle, expecting her to be pleased. "She laughed so hard," he said, "she sat down on a bucket." When she finally got her breath back she gasped out, "It looks like a tombstone."

John Paul flickered his pale glance at me. "And that's exactly what it was," he said.

Agnes died in a hospital in Seattle after an operation. The last time he saw her, just before his ship sailed, she made him promise never to have anything to do with another woman. At first, John Paul did not worry much about this vow. As he explained, any man would make a promise like that, out of kindness, if a woman lay dying. But little by little, after her death, a strange feeling had come over him. Fearful things happened every time he got himself a girl. Once there was an angry husband and a knife right through his neck. Then he was thrown into that crummy jail in Chile and another time he woke up in an alley in Hong Kong, rolled of everything he had, even his shoes gone.

"That wasn't Agnes," I could not help bursting out. "If you'd gone out with decent girls, you wouldn't have got into such messes."

But John Paul claimed he had actually *heard* Agnes.

"I've heard her a lot," he said somberly. "All over the world." One early morning in San Francisco, for example, weaving back to his ship after a night on the town, her wild sea bird's laugh struck right out at him from the fog, just before he stepped into the street and was hit by a taxi. "That time I ended up in the hospital for six weeks."

Each fresh encounter turned out worse than the last. As John Paul worded it, "She was working up to something." Finally he could not stand it any more and took to shunning women. "Living like a monk," he said. Even when his ship called at some balmy port and lights shining out across a bay promised joy to other men, John Paul would say, "I'll just stay by the ship." The only time he left it was to nip out for a haircut and back again, as fast as he could make it.

Other seamen were everlastingly kidding him about his attitude. Once, hoping to startle him, they stole a Coca-Cola ad from a drug store and stuck it up in his cabin. If they expected him to be annoyed, they were disappointed. "You know," John Paul said, "I kind of liked her." Every night, before he went to sleep, he would see her there smiling at him and when he woke up in the morning, she would still be standing there and smiling. Finally he came to think of her as his good angel. When he changed ships, he took the cardboard girl with him, strapped to the side of his taxi.

The Coca-Cola ad had been his only female companion for a number of years when his ship called at Coos Bay and as usual he whipped out for a haircut. But this trip turned out not to be usual at all. Crossing a street in the center of town he had seen his cardboard girl in the flesh. Or one so like her it made no difference. Same dark hair, same big brown eyes, and after he had followed her and picked her up (which I gathered had not been too difficult), the same smile, so dearly familiar to him. Her name was Gina Ricci. Sitting with her over a cocktail, John Paul was struck with wonder. He had only seen his cardboard girl in full face, but when Gina turned her head, for the first time he saw her in profile and her profile was exactly as he had dreamed it would be. It was a wonder, too, to see the different expressions on her face. Not always the smile, but a lip thrust out now and then in a pout or wrinkling up her nose when she was being funny. Even her voice sounded familiar to him. He listened hungrily to every word she said, trying to catch up with the things which had been happening to her in real life while he had been loving only the image of her.

Little by little, he had experienced a great sense of freedom, too. As he had it figured out, Gina was his good angel and, with her, he was rid of Agnes at last. He had left his ship immediately and taken a job at the Ticoma in order to be near her.

"Had she posed for the ad?" I asked, but John Paul shook his head. Nothing as commonplace as all that, I gathered. Finding his cardboard girl was another proof of the strangeness of life and of the mysterious way a man's destiny came to meet him. A miracle was the only word for it, he said. For a moment he sat still, jabbing a potato with his knife, while melancholy settled over him again. "She won't say she'll marry me," he said at last, sounding baffled, as if he were puzzling in his mind over a miracle which had so serious a flaw.

I tried to decide if John Paul was an unattractive man and decided no—he was not really unattractive, except for all those tattoos. He was well built, lean, with a way of moving which suggested an athlete. And there were some girls, I had heard, who got quite excited about tattoos, but his habit of silence might put a girl off unless she were the noisy type herself who would like a sounding board.

When I asked him about Gina's job he hedged a little, telling me she didn't have a job yet. She, too, had only recently arrived in Coos Bay. Since he sounded so evasive about this, I decided he must be keeping her, an impression which was strengthened when I ran into John Paul and Gina in Coos Bay during my first weekend off.

To some people, I suppose, Coos Bay would not seem to be a particularly exciting place, just a busy little fishing port and lumber center where smells of the sea and forest mingle and with a population of some five thousand souls, back then in the late forties. To me, after two weeks in the woods, it looked like Paris.

I will never again listen incredulously to tales of a logger's rip-roaring sprees in town, of the irresponsible throwing away of money earned by hard work in the woods. I felt irresponsible myself that first day in town. Old Fox drove me down from camp; I checked in at the Tioga Hotel and there I was, with a weekend on my hands and my two weeks' draw to spend if I wanted.

First I opened an account at the bank and then sent off a check to El, Ole and Knute in San Francisco, for presents. After that I hurried happily around, spending money like a drunken logger, principally on summer dresses, the prettiest of which I put right on and wore for the rest of the day.

I haven't had so much fun since the pigs ate my little brother, I thought, peering into my purse. Seeing a ten-dollar bill there, I rushed into a beauty shop. After the overpowering male atmosphere of the logging camp, that quite ordinary beauty shop seemed to me to be the most delightful spot in the world. I stood for a moment, sniffing its lovely smells of perfume, hair lotions and creams and then I climbed into a pink leather chair and gave myself over to the flattering solicitude of the operator.

It was after six when I finally stepped out again into the street, planning to have dinner in a restaurant and then go to a movie. The daytime shopping crowd had thinned out and the town had not yet worked up to its evening festivities. The only person I saw near at hand was the logger, Ed, whose full name I had learned was Edison Smith. He stopped when he saw me, said "Hi," and then, as he came a little closer, grinned and gave a low admiring whistle. Not because I was the only woman for miles around, either, I thought with satisfaction. Coos Bay must be full of girls, most of whom would be pleased enough to get a whistle out of Edison Smith. He looked as if he were fresh from the barber and he was dressed as he had been in Fleishacker Zoo, in a green gabardine cruiser outfit, the most becoming outfit a man can wear, in my opinion.

When he asked me to go to dinner with him I knew right away that nothing but a date with a logger could finish my first day off in the proper style. Fifteen minutes later I was sitting with him in a restaurant, digging into a seafood dinner, delicious in its own right and positively epicurean to me since I had had no hand in its preparation. I had carefully avoided both Edison Smith and Wild Bill ever since their dramatic return to camp. A churlish attitude on my part I realized now, examining with admiration the rugged face and good bones of the man across the table from me.

The restaurant was perched on a cliff overlooking the ocean and from our table by the window we looked out over breakers, tipped with gold as the sun dropped lower. When even the afterglow was gone, the light from Cape Arago lighthouse kept cutting through the darkness. A few couples were dancing and I braced myself for a vigorous experience as I started off with Edison, expecting a dance with a logger to be a boisterous affair, probably with much stamping of the feet. Instead, I discovered Edison could have danced circles around most of the men I knew in San Francisco.

"You logger boys have some hidden talents," I told him when we got back to our table.

"I was a Minnesota wheat farmer before I was a logger," Edison said, "and Minnesota wheat farmers are apt to be pretty catty on their feet." As he explained, the farms there were a good distance apart so the farmers held dances at the drop of a hat. Edison was dancing by the time he was eight. "And even before that," he said, "I can remember lying on a bench in a Grange hall watching while Mother and Dad danced."

He was still a farmer at heart and logging only a part-time job with him. When he had first come out from Minnesota, before the price of lumber skyrocketed, he had picked up three hundred and sixty acres of timberland on the Millicoma for a tree farm, some of it logged off and some ready to harvest. His logging wages went into its development.

The evening was a companionable one. I can talk farm with the best of them. The memories came washing back to me and I launched into a tale of the three years I tried to run a farm myself, a little place my father had picked up on a bad mortgage. "I patched the roof and mended the fence and my herd of cattle grew to seven, too," I said, feeling proud of myself for a minute. Then I added, "I couldn't bear to sell any of them to be butchered, so I ended up picking ferns and huckleberry brush to buy hay and grain for the critters."

"So the farm wasn't a success, I take it," Edison said.

"It was a complete flop," I told him. The first, I remembered, of a whole series of flops, running right on through the years and ending with Doug Weatherby and my most abysmal failure of all. I suppose the memory of all those defeats was mirrored for a moment in my face.

"People can get it in the neck and still not be licked," Edison said gently.

I picked up my highball glass. "To the undefeated," I said. Words do queer things to me. Simply saying "undefeated" out loud made me feel adventurous all at once, as if the mess in my past were a matter of gaining experience, instead of a pattern set for my entire future life, as I sometimes suspected.

We ran into John Paul and Gina Ricci quite late in the evening, while Edison was dropping me off at the Tioga Hotel. She did look remarkably like his Coca-Cola ad, too. Only not half so innocent, I thought when John Paul introduced her. What impressed me most about the meeting was John Paul and the way he reflected every expression of hers during the moment we all stood there together. When she smiled politely so did he. When she stopped smiling he seemed to be waiting almost breathlessly for the next expression to chase itself across her face. She was little and thin and she glanced at me with a hesitant, uncertain air and at Edison with a slow appraisal before she dragged John Paul away.

She is a pretty thing, I said to myself, looking after them. Her hair was as crisp as a little black goat's fleece. There was even something about her walk which reminded me of a little goat's prance. But when I remembered the look of awakened happiness in John Paul's eyes, I had some qualms. Gina had not looked to me as if she would be any man's good angel.

chapter five

INDIAN JOHNNY was standing outside the cookhouse looking up at the sun. Even that early in the morning it was a scorching hot sun and saffron hued from the dust in the air. I saw Johnny shake his head. He stooped over, picked up a handful of needles from under the tree by the cookhouse steps and crushed them between his fingers. When he stood up he stared out over the stands of Douglas fir with a measuring expression.

I had seen the same look in the eyes of the other loggers that morning. Low humidity means high fire danger and the hygrometer was hovering around 35°. The loggers had eaten their breakfast in stolid silence and packed their lunch buckets with none of the usual horseplay. Fire is the great nightmare of the logging camps. Most of the men had known someone killed or injured in a forest fire. Nobody who has lived through one can ever forget it.

After Indian Johnny left I picked up a handful of needles myself. They were so dry they powdered to dust in my hands.

Old Fox and Camp Push were still sitting at the breakfast table when I went back into the cookhouse.

"Do you boys want some more coffee?" I asked.

" 'Boys', she says." Old Fox looked pleased.

"Maybe she wants a raise," Camp Push said, glancing up in his usual shy fashion. But neither of them remembered to answer my question about coffee. "I had no business sending the men out this morning," Camp Push told Old Fox.

"It's not your fault, Push. I checked the hygrometer at six and it was 47°."

"At least they'll get in a few hours' work," Camp Push said. "The bastards are sure grouchy when they don't."

I went back to the pieboard to start my pies. Fifteen minutes later, Old Fox came into the kitchen. "We're on Hoot Owl," he told Meatball.

"Hoot Owl already?" Meatball exploded. "It's still early summer."

"As of now, we're on Hoot Owl," Old Fox repeated decisively. "If we don't get the crew spooling along by daybreak we're sunk. We're behind in our orders already."

Right then I began to learn how tough logging-camp life can be. Hoot Owl meant loggers getting up at two in the morning to be in the woods, ready to roll at the first crack of dawn, hoping to put in a few hours' work before the humidity dropped to the danger point. According to Oregon law, all logging stops when the humidity drops to 30°. Then a spark from a chain saw or from steel striking against bare rock can turn thousands of acres of timber into a monstrous thundering torch. Moonshine Jake even claimed he had seen rotten logs explode by themselves when the humidity was down to 14°.

"What you mean is," Mike Torbin said, "you were dragging a cable across a log and the friction set it off."

"The hell it did," Moonshine Jake growled. "That log exploded by itself. I tell you I was an eyeball witness."

The whole camp was out of kilter. Poker games were in progress at all hours of the day and night. And in the cookhouse we were the walking dead within three days. Men ate straight around the clock, mechanics, carpenters and truck drivers at their regular hours, loggers whenever they came in from the woods. We in the kitchen crew slept when we got a chance, which was not often. We slept in snatches, in relays, just so the table was always set and food ready for the hungry.

To make matters worse, Meatball was in a state of deep indignation. Some of the men, with too much time on their hands, wired his iron bedstead to a live battery and coil. When Meatball slumped exhausted onto his electrified bed, it took seconds before his tired brain reacted to his rump's warning and he leaped yelling out of the door. He was met by a loud horselaugh from the men, watching through a crack in the bunkhouse.

Meatball immediately charged over to the cookhouse and, with his jutting eyebrows pulled down almost to his nose, went about dumping extra handfuls of salt into the kettle of navy beans and hambones which the men particularly relished. In this he was within his rights. The crew recognized it as a fair retaliation, but it did not make for good feeling.

As for me, I was groping around half blind, so bushed I couldn't think about anything except how much I wanted to go to sleep.

Every day Old Fox, seeing our demoralized faces, would swear with a big oath to bring us another flunkey within twenty-four hours. Five days went by and no flunkey appeared. And then one afternoon I staggered back to the cookhouse, still only half awake, to find Meatball's face wonderfully cleared. "We've got another flunkey," he said. "Lee, meet your new roommate. John Paul's fiancée."

Gina Ricci was standing by the door, looking marvelously demure. John Paul loomed anxiously behind her. How he had wangled Gina into the job I will never know. I don't believe she had ever been in a kitchen before, let alone a cookhouse. That was all right with me. I absolutely beamed at her—not only because she was another hand to peel potatoes and carry plates, either. Meatball had said "fiancée," so she must be planning to marry John Paul after all. A satisfactory situation—I do not like miracles to have flaws in them.

"Mama mia!" Gina cried out when she saw the Old Homestead. She clattered up the steps and ran all around the cabin, peering into every corner. Then she darted out the door and ran around the outside. "A whole little house and only one room!" To her New York-bred eyes, this strange fact seemed to make up for its ramshackle appearance. "I've seen them like this in the movies," she said happily.

The very next day I woke from a nap to a wonderful freshness in the air. Even my skin felt different and when I looked out I could see a breeze riffling the tops of the trees. The humidity was up to 50°, Meatball's eyebrows were back to normal position and we were off Hoot Owl. But Gina Ricci stayed on.

So I was no longer the only woman in camp and glad of it, too. Nothing but hairy cheeks, rumbling voices and men swaggering around can become almost unbearable after a while, no matter how much you admire the brutes. It is like listening to an orchestra made up entirely of brasses and drums and never the sound of a woodwind to soften the general uproar. Eventually it hurts your ears.

Occasionally I have read stories written by some woman who has paid a visit to the ranch country or some other predominantly male environment. She usually thinks the social gatherings there are screamingly funny, especially the way the men collect at one end of the hall while the wives flock together at the other. By the exercise of great tact, she finally gets the two groups to *mix,* and thinks she has done something very smart, too.

As a matter of fact the last thing those wives wanted was to play parlor games with *men,* for heaven's sake, when they came all the way into town. Men they had in their hair all the time. The fun of a party was the company of other women. The wives must have wanted to wring the neck of that outlander, spoiling all the sport with her corny notions about parlor games and mixing.

With Gina sharing the Old Homestead, I could borrow bobby pins again, and talk to someone who knew passionate pink was a shade of lipstick and not a violent political opinion. I also found I was now the old settler, the experienced hand—a new and invigorating feeling to me. It built up my ego. Very soon I discovered something else. When I first arrived at the Ticoma camp, it had seemed to me the back of nowhere, shut off from the world by millions of feet of Douglas fir. Instead, I found out that the Ticoma logging camp *was* the world, in a more vital way than I had ever known the world before. No doubt dramatic things happened in San Francisco, but I had been struggling so hard to write novels and to get Doug Weatherby to want to marry me and feeling so sorry for myself that I had missed them all. At the Ticoma, being one of sixty humans tossed down together in the center of the forest, the dramas played themselves out right in front of my nose. The first of these was the drama of Gina.

Gina had come to the United States from Italy as a small child and had lived ever since in New York City. Finally a friend—male, I am sure—offered to drive her to the Pacific Coast. They had reached Seattle before she discovered he was driving a stolen car. When the police took him in, Gina had grabbed a bus going south, heading vaguely toward Hollywood alone. Her money took her only as far as Coos Bay. She had been looking about for a lift the rest of the way when she met John Paul, and he had finally argued her into taking a job at the Ticoma.

If you could call it a job. Gina did not take her duties in the cookhouse very seriously. She spent more time feeding leftover pie to the pigs than she did preparing vegetables. Meatball would roll his eyes heavenward in exasperation as she rattled around the kitchen. She would start into the lunchroom with a platter of cold meat and then set it on the chopping block instead, while she rushed outdoors to watch the Forest Service Plane fly overhead. But nobody complained. The cookhouse had never run more smoothly. John Paul did the work for both of them. He worked like a coal heaver, one eye on his own job and one on Gina's. They would sit together on the cookhouse steps, peeling potatoes or scraping carrots, Gina chattering and fooling along, John Paul watching her, rapt, as if he were a man touched by glory.

As far as the loggers were concerned, she behaved herself well, recognizing the interest of the younger men with only the ghost of a smile and a dark sideways glint of eyes. During the evening coffee sessions, she stuck close to John Paul. And to do them justice, the loggers seemed to accept her status as John Paul's girl and made very little effort to muscle in.

It was nearly a week before she began to look down in the mouth. She was sitting cross-legged on our wooden slab when I came in one afternoon. "All the bosses are married," she burst out at me.

"Yes, all married," I told her.

Gina thrust out her underlip and gave herself an annoyed twitch. "I came up here because I thought I would meet a rich one," she said, and looked at me accusingly, as if I were part of a general setup bent on thwarting her.

"Why, but you're engaged to John Paul."

Gina lifted her shoulders in a gesture of great boredom and let them drop again with a tired sigh. I sat down on the steps, feeling downhearted, too, and worried. Nobody can see intensity of feeling, like John Paul's, being wasted without regret.

Gina wrapped her arms around her knees and rocked back and forth, saying, "Damn, damn, damn."

I guess she had heard about the great lumber tycoons of the West and supposed that a logging camp was the place to find these desirable items.

At the moment, her head was outlined against lines of clothes, hung out to dry. There were always lines of bright washing flapping around the shack now, Gina's pajamas, heavily loaded with lace, her panties and slips and dresses, all in vivid reds and oranges and greens. The Old Homestead had taken on the gay, light-hearted air of a carnival tent, surrounded by banners and pennants. Dr. Freud probably would have had a few words to say about Gina's passion for cleanliness. She used to bathe (at our cold-water sink) and change all her clothes from the skin out three times a day. Whenever I came into the Old Homestead there she would be, busily washing out her clothes.

"That Camp Push," she said finally, "he's cute."

I never would have called our big, quiet Push "cute," but he was certainly a likeable man.

"When I first came," she said, "I was thinking about that Camp Push and then I hear he's married, so I say,

'Please, God, put him out of my mind.'" She shrugged her shoulders again. "Mike Torbin, he's married, too!"

"He's married and he's got nine children," I snapped. Mike was the young, very handsome cat skinner, completely devoted to his family, and harboring the fierce ambition to be as great a cat skinner as Wild Bill some day.

"Now look," I said, trying not to sound too top lofty, "John Paul is absolutely crazy about you and he's a nice guy. You could look a long way before you could find anybody who loved you as much as he does."

"He's always wanting me to go out in his car and park. He says he bought it just because of me." She made a face, as if she had a bad taste in her mouth and subsided into a dark brooding. When she spoke again, it was in a breathless whisper. "What is it keeps watching in the woods?"

"There's nothing watching," I said. "Oh, a squirrel, maybe, or a chipmunk." But I knew what she meant. Anyone who has walked through the deep Oregon woods knows the feeling, as if a presence were there, silent but aware. Maybe it is only the multitude of little living things, the gnats and the spiders and the shrews, taking note of your passing. But sometimes I have imagined that the trees themselves have a consciousness or that the whole forest is a single entity. We who were born near the woods are used to the feeling of a presence there and know it is not unfriendly. Just aloof. But Gina had never been away from New York City and I think she felt the true panic terror.

The sight of any wild thing frightened her. The whisk of a squirrel's tail around the trunk of a tree or a rustling in the leaves made her shy like a horse, her eyes showing their whites and her shoulders tense.

"There is something in the woods that watches," she repeated stubbornly.

Now the hogs enchanted her. Before long Gertie and her brood of pigs took to following her around as much as they did Meatball. She was generally good for a handout. And a quaint parade they made, too, Gina prancing along at the head of the line, looking over her shoulder and crowing with delight at sight of all those little pigs with their pink noses and corkscrew tails scampering along behind her. She looked about ten years old at such times.

When she was sleeping, she looked younger than that. About seven, I would have said. She always took a baby doll to bed with her. It was an old doll, dating back to her childhood, I imagine, with a plaster head and body and a nose which had been broken off at some time in its history.

"What happened to his nose?" I asked one night.

Gina flashed immediately into a rage. "Oh, that brute of a man," she cried. She snatched up the doll and kissed it fiercely. The paint was already off its face, probably due to just such paroxysms of kissing.

This great brute of a man, she said (actually trembling with fury at the memory), had rolled over on the doll in bed and its arm had stuck into him. So he had jerked it out from under the covers and thrown it across the room. "Can you imagine?" she said, outraged. "An innocent little thing like that? It had never hurt nobody. Nobody, nobody."

I made a sympathetic sound and Gina blazed on. She followed the man home, she said, to find out where he lived and the next day bribed the janitor to let her into the beast's room. "And I cut up all his suits with a razor."

Old Fox would have been very startled if he knew a little more about the new flunkey, I imagined. "John Paul's fiancée" probably sounded extremely respectable to him.

For a minute I wondered how much John Paul knew about her life. Everything no doubt. He wouldn't care.

I believe she might have liked John Paul better if he had not tried so desperately to please her. She had taken to baiting him. One of her jobs was to help him clean up after meals. When the loggers had scraped and stacked their own plates on the cart near the dining-room door and dropped their silverware through a hole into sudsy water, John Paul wheeled the cart into the kitchen and ran the dishes through three waters, first in a sink with detergent powder, next in one with disinfectant and finally in a clear, steaming rinse. After they were stacked in a wooden drainer, he set a steel dishpan of water on the stove, added soap powder and boiled the silverware for several minutes. When it had been rinsed three or four times he folded a white blanket in half, spread it on a table and dumped the silverware onto it.

He would take one end of the blanket and Gina the other and between them they would rock it back and forth until the silverware was dry and twinkling. Except every now and then Gina would drop her end and let the silverware clatter all over the floor. Then she'd stand there, grinning impishly, while John Paul crawled around picking up knives and forks. He would have done better to have swatted her. Naturally, the silverware had to be boiled and dried over again.

I believe he even handed over most of his paycheck to her. One weekend we rode to town together. After losing so much time while the camp was on Hoot Owl, the woods bosses were feeling pressed to get orders filled and Old Fox had begun to hire more men. They were even working Saturdays, so Gina and I had to stay and help with the breakfast. Swivelneck was slated to drive us to Coos Bay and promptly at nine o'clock we climbed into the commissary truck and started off.

Ever since the episode of the pinch, the relationship between Swivelneck and me had been constrained. He always acted excessively dignified whenever I was about. "I'll have to stop up Canyon Creek on our way to watch the road crew for an hour or so," he said, when we drove away from camp. I wanted to see the works anyway, so the idea of the side trip pleased me. "They're using three times too much dynamite," he went on, as we jogged up a rocky road along Canyon Creek. "I've told Old Fox so, too. They leave boxes all over the woods. Too damn lazy to dig it out when it doesn't go off."

I knew the men resented Swivelneck's prowling around the works. In their opinion, his place was in the office. As they frequently remarked, if Old Fox and Camp Push were satisfied, Swivelneck could damn well mind his own business. During nightly coffee sessions I heard them saying, "Wouldn't it be real amazing if a log happened to roll on that so-and-so sometime?" Or, "What a pure shame if Swivelneck should happen to get too close to a blast."

I felt embarrassed at being along on his snooping, although it was fun to watch Wild Bill riding his mighty Cat. To my romantic mind he looked like a conquering hero, sitting up ramrod straight as the monster plunged ahead, shouldering aside broken lengths of logs, big stumps and boulders as large as the commissary truck. The man and the Cat together might have come straight out of heroic legend.

Edison Smith was spending the weekend at his farm so Moonshine Jake was chasing Cat for Wild Bill. According to regulations, no cat skinner can go into the woods without his chaser, who blasts stumps and rocks out of the way, bucks logs too big for the Cat to shove and tends the safety line, on which the cat skinner's life often depends. The safety line is a winch line, a cable on a powered drum at the back of the Cat, something like a fishing line and reel. The cat chaser ties one end of it around a tree whenever the Cat is in a tricky place. It rides loose until the cat skinner is in danger and then he puts the winch in gear and reels the cable tight, to keep the Cat from going over the cliff. Wild Bill was working close to the creek's steep bank, and Moonshine Jake, I noticed, kept a close watch on the safety line, fastened to a tree.

"There's one stump he won't push over," Swivelneck said, pointing. "They'll have to dynamite."

When Wild Bill reached the stump, some five feet in diameter, he backed up close to us and shut off the Cat, while Jake got ready to blast. Ever since my date with Edison, Wild Bill's attitude toward me had changed drastically. No devilish glint in his green eyes at all. Just a studied brotherly attitude.

Gina sat up, stiff and mad looking, and gave him the evil eye. From the amused quirk of Wild Bill's mouth, I suspected some slight hugger-mugger between the two. A still hunt, probably, on Gina's part which had not come off. Wild Bill was a very wise bird.

Moonshine Jake began to haul equipment out of a nearby machine, a "half track," with truck wheels in front and Cat-like tracks, but with rubber pads, in back. He took out two poles, a roll of ropey black wire and a box of dynamite. Since I had used such boxes to sit on, as a dresser and to keep my cosmetics in, I watched carefully to see how the contents worked.

First Jake jabbed between the roots with a bull-prick, until he had made a hole directly under the stump. Then, with his jackknife, he cut a length as long as his arm from the ropey bundle and fastened a fuse and cap to it. After that he kicked open the box of dynamite with his calk boot, took out a stick and broke it in half. When he had made a pocket in the half stick, he inserted the cap, gave the fuse a half hitch around the stick and poked it carefully under the stump with a wooden rod they called a loading stick. After he had kicked the hole full of dirt and tamped it down with the loading stick, a small snake of fuse still stuck out. Finally he lit the fuse and stepped back three or four feet. After a few seconds, there was a disappointing little "poof."

"Well, that was a comedown," I said.

"The hole it made under the stump is exactly where it belongs," Wild Bill told me.

Jake was busy cleaning out the enlarged hole with the bull-prick. He poked half a box of dynamite under the stump, one stick at a time, attached a cap and about fifteen feet of fuse to a stick which he shoved in, too, and finally loaded in the rest of the dynamite. When he had tamped the dirt over the hole the fuse stretched along the ground like a lurking serpent.

"Back up," he yelled at Swivelneck and Bill. "Better back up to the corner." He pointed to a bend in the road some four hundred feet away. Swivelneck backed the entire distance, but Wild Bill left the Cat halfway and walked back to the downed log beside the commissary truck, where Gina and I sat for a better view.

Jake took his time about getting the lunch buckets out of the half truck. "Here's your lunch, Bill," he said as he joined us. "Might as well get it et." He began spreading out his lunch on the log, ignoring the lighted fuse.

Several minutes passed while I waited tensely for the

big boom. "Do you think we're far enough away?" I asked nervously.

"Sure. Nothing but a little bitty old chip could come this far," Jake assured me.

Minutes went ticking by.

"It's not going off, Jake," Swivelneck said finally. "That's where all the powder waste comes in."

"Keep your shirt on, you smug bastard. It ain't time."

"You'll keep on saying that until we get tired of waiting," Swivelneck said. "I'm not leaving until I see you dig that back up."

Jake shrugged and sipped his coffee lustily. He winked at Gina and me.

Swivelneck's face kept getting redder. Finally he jumped up and started toward the stump.

"Sit down!" Jake bellowed.

Swivelneck backed up and sat down. In a few more seconds, Jake said, "You can go now, if you want to."

Swivelneck had taken about ten steps when the earth was filled with a trembling rumble, the air exploded, a black cloud swirled to envelop us, myriads of flying chips rained down and I covered my face with my hands. Jake was slapping his thighs in mirth, while Swivelneck backed slowly toward the truck, his face as grey as the acrid smoke drifting lazily from the yawning hole.

"By jingo, I went and timed that a wee bit wrong," Jake howled gleefully.

"Let's get to town, you two," Swivelneck growled.

The man had gone out of his way to irritate everybody, I knew, but still I did not think the dynamite trick a very funny one. Gina, however, was convulsed with laughter. All the way to town she kept looking sideways at Swivelneck, humped over the wheel, and then she would double up again.

She surely had John Paul's paycheck as well as her own to spend that weekend in town. When she came back to the Old Homestead on Sunday evening, she was staggering under packages and boxes. More lace panties, more purple brassieres, more satin lounging robes (and who could lounge at the Ticoma?), piles of junk jewelry, bracelets, necklaces and earrings (which she later fastened to the pigs' tails), bedroom slippers trimmed with maribou, and three evening gowns, all of them too tight for her. Or so I thought. Gina seemed to think they fitted perfectly.

The only purchase I thoroughly approved of was a little music box. She played it every chance she had and another tune would have driven me crazy. But this was charming, with a lilt to it and yet a stately elegance, too. Perhaps it was a gavotte. I seemed to hear the rustle of silk and the trip of dancing feet. Gina would play it, sitting in her favorite position, cross-legged on our chopping block. The part she particularly loved was the end, when the box ran down and the tune came slower and slower and began to fade away. There would be a few lingering silver tinkles and finally silence. But after the silence had lasted a second or two, if you listened carefully, you could hear one last little note, hardly more than a ghost of a sound.

"Oh, so sad! So sad!" Gina would cry, looking perfectly delighted, and she would snatch up the box and wind it again. There really was something satisfying about that last faint sound, coming as it did after the tune had died away. I found myself listening for it. As if it were a sigh or the memory of a lost love.

chapter six

LOGGERS are continually risking their necks. A choker setter, for example, is wary every time he races under a taut cable to fasten the choker to a log. Many a snapped cable has broken a leg or severed a neck. A high climber, working his way up a tree to cut off its limbs and top it, courts death at every upward toss of his belt and at every swing of his ax which could sever the steel core of the safety rope. A runaway log or a wavering tree can mean death to a faller or bucker. Loggers have a name for limbs torn loose and lodged high in a tree. They call them "widow makers."

Nothing so electrifies a camp as the steady blast of the donkey whistle. Sometimes at the Ticoma, the men would be working too far away from camp for us to hear the whistle. Then the first warning that something was wrong would be the sound of heavy boots clumping across the bridge. That sound will strike terror to my heart to my dying day.

A side always stopped work when a logger was hurt and the men plodded back to camp on foot while the crummy which they had ridden out to the job would be used to haul the injured man to town or down the road until it met the ambulance. The Fire Patrol Station near camp had the only communication system within reach. When a logger was seriously injured, the Fire Warden would radio to Coos Bay for an ambulance.

If a man was just banged up, he would be brought into the kitchen for first aid. A cook is expected to be handy in any emergency, but Meatball fainted at the sight of human blood so, as second cook, the job of binding up the wounds fell to me. At last some use was being made of those unhappy months I spent in nurses' training, I used to think as I washed and swabbed with antiseptic and bandaged.

The crew took it for granted that accidents would always happen in triplicate. As far as the Ticoma went, the old superstition seemed well founded. One day Snoozy grabbed onto an electric wire he had meant to disconnect and all but electrocuted himself before John Paul could race to the power shack and pull the generator switch. The next day a choker setter slipped as he was about to set the tongs into a peeled log and broke his leg.

The following morning, Friday the thirteenth, to boot, gloom hung over the breakfast tables. The racket of the loggers' departure was subdued enough to be ominous. Even in the kitchen we were jumpy, with Meatball grouching when my berry pies boiled over. I was taking the hateful things out of the oven when, off in the distance, we heard the heavy tread of boots on the wooden bridge and all ran to the door. The men were plodding toward us, their eyes on the dust and their shoulders stooped.

Like a sleepwalker, Wild Bill crossed the dining room and slumped onto a bench. He stretched his arms out on the table, put his head down on them and sat shaking.

Meatball got out his cooking brandy and poured a water tumbler full. "Drink it," he said.

Wild Bill shook his head.

Meatball shoved the glass at him and after a moment

Bill lifted his head and drained it without a breath. "We couldn't even pick him up," he said hoarsely. "The ambulance is going to bring up some orderlies. All mangled to hell. We couldn't even pick him up."

Edison Smith had dropped onto the bench beside Wild Bill. I took one look at his white face, reached for Meatball's bottle and poured him out a hearty slug, too.

"Who?" Meatball asked.

"Mike," Wild Bill burst out. "Mike Torbin. With a wife and nine kids. Goddamn it, that's who."

My own knees felt weak and I sat down heavily across the table from them.

"It was that new chaser he had." Wild Bill slapped the table with the palm of his hand. "I'll kill the son of a bitch if we ever find him. He took off down the road, the yellow dog. I should've gone after him. I'd of killed him sure." A little color was coming back into his face.

"Know what a safety line is on a Cat?" Edison asked.

I nodded.

"Well," he said, "instead of being up there by the tree where the safety line was fastened, watching, like he should have been, this new chaser of Mike's was goofing off somewhere. There's a big clevis—a U-shaped piece of metal with holes in each end to hold a pin—well this bum had used a pin that had the threads stripped."

"He'd put the pin upside down in the clevis," Bill said. "I'll kill the damn fool. The first pull of the winch the pin fell out. Mike was way out on the cliff and he kept shaking the clutch gear like he couldn't believe the line wasn't tightening. I yelled and yelled for him to reverse, but he couldn't hear."

Bill took a deep breath. "Five hundred feet down that goddamn cliff. We couldn't even pick him up."

Meatball motioned to me and I went into the kitchen. "It's almost lunchtime," he said.

"They won't eat, will they?"

"Not likely," Meatball said. "But we'd better have all the coffee boilers full. I think we could make a big kettle of tomato soup, too. It might tempt a few of them. They need something in their stomachs."

Meatball was right. All the men who came in drank coffee and a few hardy souls even had a bowl of soup. There was only a heavy silence in the dining room until I heard Snoozy, the bull cook, talking. "It'll be days before the State Accident gets any money to her. Today's payday, but she can't cash his check and Old Fox is up north."

Pretty soon he came into the kitchen, shouting over his shoulder, "You guys go after your money if you haven't any with you." He handed me his hat. "Pass this around as soon as all these lugs get back here. His wife'll need someone to stay with the little tykes. There's a baby, too, and I know they lived from payday to payday. Probably not a scrap of food in the house, nor any oil for the stove, either. Besides, she'll need clothes for the funeral."

After I had made the rounds, we dumped the contents of the hat onto the serving counter and toted it up while the crew watched from the dining room. I found a fifty dollar check from Snoozy, a great many twenties and a few tens. It totaled $540. "If the whole crew had been here, that poor woman could have paid off the mortgage," Meatball said.

Whenever there had been an accident in camp and tension built up, the men played poker harder and longer. After Mike Torbin's death, poker was the only thing anybody talked about. They seemed to submerge themselves completely in runs and flushes and tales of fabulous hands. And all at once Gina was wonderfully gay.

Being Gina, the sudden excitement had to be caused by one of the men. I discovered which man through overhearing her carrying on a conversation with a hog.

Our hogs belonged to Hans, the road boss. Hans also had the garbage concession and had introduced the hogs into camp as a lucrative sideline. Old Fox kept trying to get rid of them. But Hans was a superb road builder. He could lay out a logging road in the most impossible places and arrive at a perfect grade without even the aid of a transit, just an engineer's level. The arguments always ended when Hans said, "Dem peegs ain't hurtin nobodies. My peegs go, I go, and dot's dot."

Gina hauled a pig out from under the Old Homestead by its hind leg one day and lugged it onto our porch, where the two of them sat on the wooden slab eating apple pie together, the pig in her lap.

"Pooh, pooh," she said, shoving her face down close to the pig's and wrinkling up her nose. "You stink." This seemed to amuse her no end. "Stinky, kinky King," she chortled and glanced up at me, sideways from under her eyelashes. "You know that King?"

It took me a second to think whom she was talking about. "That new man, Al King?"

She gave a whoop of laughter. "Stinky, kinky King," she caroled again to the pig.

Al King drove the water wagon—the sprinkler which kept down the dust on the roads. He had been in camp about a week and he certainly was not stinky. Quite the opposite—a clean-looking man, with curly light hair cut short all over his head and a boyish smile. Yet he must have done something pretty bad for Gina to name a pig after him, I decided.

Gina reached over and scratched the pig's belly, made another face at it, as if she were smelling something unpleasant, and finally spanked its rump. "You old dirty King," she said.

I sat down on the steps, suddenly sobered. She was not insulting King at all, with this byplay over the pig. It was a passionate endearment. The psychology was over my head, but there was no mistaking her red-hot excitement.

"Oops," she cried, jumping up and dumping the pig off her lap to shake out her skirts. "King has wet his pants." This, too, seemed to delight her.

"What's this Al King like?" I asked Edison Smith that night. Edison had taken to strolling around to the cookhouse every evening and I had come to watch for him.

"King?" Edison's expression was startled and a little worried as he studied my face. He thinks I'm interested myself and he doesn't like it, I thought.

"King's a boomer," he said. "One of these guys with itchy feet who can't stay anywhere more than a month or two. He's worked in half the logging camps and construction jobs on the coast. Makes out all right, I guess. He seems to be loaded."

Snoozy butted into the conversation at this point and said Al King was not going to be loaded much longer, not after these sharpies got through with him, he wasn't. Al King, it seemed, couldn't keep away from the poker tables and he was a continual loser. "That wad of his will sure slim up," Snoozy said. "He's one of these stubborn cusses. He don't know yet luck's something you can't stare down. I've seen them before. Just too damn sure they're right."

Very little around camp escaped Snoozy's popping, inquisitive eyes. "I told him so, too," he went on. "I said, 'You better get wise to yourself, young feller, or these guys will have your shirt.' That's what I told him, but he said you had to ride down your tough luck just like a bronc stomper. Pretty soon, he said, you'd have it following along behind you and whinnying. He claims he's played with experts and cleaned them out. That I'd like to see."

Al King himself seldom came to the cookhouse. When he did, it was to gulp down a cup of coffee, say a breezy thank you and get on back to the bosses' cabin and the poker tables. He came in quite late that night and from the general air of congratulation, I gathered his luck had begun to change at last.

"They're just fattening you up for the kill," Snoozy warned him and King gave him an even white smile. On the surface, he and Gina ignored each other. While he was there, Gina made a big point of teasing John Paul, flirting with him in such an exaggerated way that it became a mockery, while King watched with an amused grin. And if John Paul ever catches on, I thought, and checked myself. John Paul had already caught on. He looked like a baited bear.

That was when I began to worry. John Paul did not seem to me the type of man who could be pushed too far. And Gina began to get reckless. Once I woke in the middle of the night and saw the moonlight washing through the windows and over Gina's bed, rumpled but empty except for the baby doll tossed on the pillow. For a minute I lay there, conscious of the silence, of the fir-scented breeze stirring our flour-sack curtains, and telling myself that Gina was a fool and there was no sense in worrying about her. When I woke again, it was morning and Gina was back in her bed, sleeping curled up like a little cat with the doll in her arms.

The next night the same thing happened. She could not have averaged more than four hours' sleep a day, including her afternoon naps, and yet she scrambled out of bed in the morning, fresh as a spring colt. "Don't you like anybody?" she asked me one afternoon, crossly, as if my uninterrupted nights bored her. She had just finished painting her toe nails and was wandering around the cabin barefooted to give them a chance to dry. "That Edison, he's crazy for you."

"What makes you think so?" I demanded.

But Gina had already lost interest. "Oh, I don't know," she said indifferently, flopping onto her cot.

I remembered the way Edison looked each evening when he came into the cookhouse and his slow smile when he caught sight of me. His smile was not a surface thing. It reached well into his eyes.

I glanced over at Gina's cot. She was already asleep. I got up softly and pulled my overnight bag out from under my bed. The portfolio was down at the bottom where I had shoved it when I packed in San Francisco. I knew without opening it exactly what it contained. A picture of Doug Weatherby and two letters from him. In my mind I could already see the vigorous handwriting. There are lots of other men in the world, I told myself, afraid for a moment to open the portfolio. Keeping these things was like refusing to bury a corpse. The life had gone out of our affair. It was high time to get rid of the bones.

Oh, but it wasn't dead. When I opened the portfolio, Doug's face looked out at me from its leather frame as dearly familiar as ever. There was strength in the face and wit. But he must be a rat, I told myself hurriedly, trying to push my way up through the flood of memories. I closed my eyes. No, he isn't a rat. For the first time since I heard of his engagement the anger and bitterness refused to come back. Just the grief.

In the end I did not destroy anything. Despising myself a little, I locked them back in the valise and lay down again on my cot. John Paul and I were both the same kind of a fool, I decided. We simply had no sense of reality. All the same, if you want a thing badly enough, it *must* mean there is a chance of getting it, I thought, just before I fell asleep.

That philosophy was not working out for John Paul. Every night, after the poker games were over, Gina sneaked out to meet her Al King. Usually I slept through her going but one night I woke up and found her sitting on her bed, trying to tell her fortunes with cards by the light of a flashlight. She had on what she called her logger's disguise, jeans, a blue shirt and a bandanna tied around her hair. A ridiculous idea. Anybody could have spotted her as a woman even at night by the way she moved, but her efforts were made particularly asinine by her high heels. She never wore flats, in or out of the cookhouse, because she said they hurt the backs of her legs.

She glanced over at me when she heard me move and said in a tense whisper, "You take the cards and tell me if tonight it's safe to go."

"I can't tell fortunes," I said, yawning.

Gina swept the cards onto the floor and sat up straight. "Wait," she said. "I'll tell." She screwed up her face in concentration and pressed the heels of her hands against her eyes. After a minute of this, she looked up doubtfully and said, "My heart says 'go,' but my head says, 'be ca-a-areful.'"

She went back to frowning concentration and finally cried out, "My heart speaks louder!"

She had jumped up and run to the door before she hesitated, standing uncertainly. "Are there bears in the woods?" she whispered.

It was a panic-stricken sound, but I was in no mood to give comfort. "Lots of bears," I told her shortly. "Cougar, too."

I heard her catch her breath. For a second she wavered, turning her head slowly and staring out the door. I could almost see her drawing into herself, terrified, before she suddenly threw back her head and darted into the night.

I listened to her swiftly fading footsteps and wished I had not told her there were bear in the woods—Gina who was afraid of a squirrel, terrified of the woods even in the daytime. It must have taken an overwhelming drive to make her dare them in the dark when even woodsmen cling close to the campfires and try to shut the forest out. Finally I got out of bed and went to the window.

A lopsided moon was in the sky. Moonlight does strange things to the forest. It makes the shadows come alive. They would stir and tremble wherever Gina looked and the little sounds would be exaggerated. She would hear the rustle of tiny paws and magnify them horribly. I hoped with all my heart that Al King would be ahead of her at their meeting place.

The sleeping camp looked very small to me that night as I peered out the window. The forest seemed to have moved in closer, pressing up against our little corner of cleared ground as if it might take it over again at any moment. There was no sign of Gina now. And yet something stirred. I saw a shadow move across a patch of moonlight, pause and move back again. When I stared hard, I could make out the lean shape of John Paul.

It wasn't the bear, I thought uneasily, which Gina had to fear that night. For a long time I watched while he prowled back and forth between the bridge and his cabin. Sometimes it seemed to me his shoulders were hunched as if he were sheltering from a high wind, even though not the slightest breeze stirred. Sometimes he would stand absolutely still, as lonely a figure as I have ever seen. It was not many hours before daylight when he finally went back into his cabin and I crawled into bed.

I was asleep when Gina came in. I roused to the clanging of my alarm clock and climbed groggily out of bed. Even cold water from the tap failed to wake me up properly.

Gina sat up in bed and began at once to sing, in a perfectly atrocious French accent, "Ta bouche a des baisers, si bons, si doux, si longs, si fous—"

"Is that what you've been doing all night?" I asked. "Learning French?"

"You know what that means? It means your mouth has kisses, so good, so sweet, so long, so cra-a-azy—"

"Yes, I know," I said.

"So cr-a-a-zy," Gina sang out, turning a somersault which brought her out of bed and into the middle of the room. "That's cute, isn't it?"

I did not think anything about the Gina–John Paul–Al King mess was cute. Snoozy, it turned out, was as worried as I was. We met him on our way to the cookhouse. Generally Snoozy had the air of a man who has suppressed some huge joke for a long time. But not that morning. He planted himself in our path and he was dead solemn. "You got to watch out for them pale-eyed men," he told Gina.

So, I thought, he too had seen John Paul waiting last night in the shadows.

To me, John Paul looked like a drowned man. Gina no longer bothered to notice him. He might not have been in the cookhouse for all the attention she paid him. She would skimp through her work after supper and then clatter back to the Old Homestead, leaving John Paul sitting alone at one end of a table, staring into his coffee cup. If I had to speak to him, I found myself raising my voice as if it would take a loud noise to get through to him.

Gina always went straight to sleep after supper and got up again to meet her Al King when the poker game was over. The poker games were running full blast and the coffee hour grew duller. If a man did come in, he would grab a cup of coffee, gulp it down and then whip back to Camp Push's cabin where the "big" game was going on. Edison told me the stakes had gradually risen until a man could really get hurt.

"What about the two-bit limit I've been hearing about?" I asked him.

"Well, so many of the guys have lost so much, they're trying to get it back fast. They voted to drop the limit for the time being."

"I hope Old Fox doesn't get wind of it," I said. "Has Al King lost his roll yet?"

"No," Edison said in a dry voice. "He's the one who's been winning."

Al King stayed clear of the cookhouse except at meals. I was not surprised, considering the dark silence which surrounded John Paul. I kept watching him uneasily myself.

It was Friday night, payday, but the men were working half days on Saturday, so no one could go to town. There was a big game going in Camp Push's cabin. Gina, as usual, had nipped over to the Old Homestead and John Paul was sitting in the dining room drinking lemonade liberally spiked with gin from a bottle I saw under the table.

Meatball and I had just about finished our work when we heard loud voices outside the cookhouse and Camp Push came marching in, followed by a crowd of loggers. "Where's that magnifying glass of yours, Meatball?" Camp Push demanded.

Meatball said it was in his cabin.

"Well, get it," Camp Push said. As Meatball hurried away, Swivelneck arrived with a two-hundred-watt bulb from the commissary and Camp Push climbed up onto a table to screw it in.

"What on earth goes on?" I whispered to Edison. Frankly, I was scared. I never have seen such mad-looking men.

"Crisis at the poker table," Edison said. His grin reassured me a little. He told me Camp Push had been playing at a table with Swivelneck, Al King, Wild Bill, Indian Johnny and Bob Botts—the donkey puncher from number three donkey. Every logger who could get in had crowded into Push's cabin.

Swivelneck had won several small pots and then he had drawn three aces. He tossed out three twenties to open and everybody stayed. Swivelneck drew two cards and Al King, Wild Bill, Bob Botts and Camp Push three each. Indian Johnny drew one. They all stayed for the first raise and then dropped out for the second. All but Swivelneck and King. Swivelneck was red in the face but he put out four twenty-dollar bills.

"I'll see you," King said, "and raise you a hundred."

"I'll call." Swivelneck's voice was shaky, but he put down four aces with a flourish.

Very nonchalantly, King laid down a small straight flush. "And then," Edison said, "he gathered up the pot and beat it out of the room. So Swivelneck grabbed the cards and began to swear they were marked."

When Meatball came rushing in with the magnifying glass, they all gathered around, shoving up close, while Camp Push examined the cards. Even with the glass it took them quite a while to find the minute depressions along the edge of each one.

Loggers have decided ideas about money, like insisting on being paid all they are worth, glorying in overtime to fatten their paychecks and choosing their own way of getting rid of it. Losing at poker they consider money well spent. If the cops take what is left late Saturday night, that is only to be expected. But let anybody try to cheat them and you have some very aroused men.

Above the general uproar and cussing, I heard Wild Bill say, "Talk about Braille! That guy must have nerve points at the ends of all his fingers." He sounded almost admiring.

"Well, aren't we a smart bunch of yahoos," Indian Johnny said and Bob Botts shouted out, "No wonder he took that water wagon job—so he can always wear gloves."

"I guess that explains why he's covered so much territory. I'll bet he's taken every logging camp on the coast," somebody said and a voice from the back of the room yelled out. "Somebody get a rope."

"None of that," Camp Push said. "The creep isn't worth it."

"He took me for $360," Bob Botts said belligerently.

"Pipe down," Camp Push told him. "You'll get it back. And now maybe we better get the limit down to two bits again."

He started toward the door, with the others pushing

along behind. "And I'll beat hell out of him," Bob Botts, a very husky young man, said.

"Suits me." Camp Push's smile was as soft as ever.

When they had all shoved through the door, I ran out and watched as they moved in a body toward Al King's cabin. All this time John Paul had not said a word. He came out and stood beside me, watching the loggers moving in a business-like group across the open area. When they reached Al King's cabin I saw them go shoving in and the light came on. The next instant there was a great milling around out in front.

"He's gone," John Paul said with an air of finality. A second later I heard somebody yell, "His car's gone, too!"

John Paul turned around and gave me a long, questioning look. I knew exactly what was in his mind. It was in mine, too. I jumped down the steps and ran toward the Old Homestead. As soon as I came in the door, I felt the emptiness. Even before I groped for the overhead light and turned it on, I knew Gina was not there. Neither were her things. Evening dresses, baby doll, high-heeled slippers—all gone. But on my powder-box dresser was the music box, with a note under it in a labored handwriting, "For you."

John Paul took it more quietly than I expected. He said nothing at all that night when I told him. He just walked into his cabin and shut the door. But by morning, he had made some curious adjustment in his mind. He looked composed. Even the drawn look of the past week had gone and in its place—well, I could have sworn it was satisfaction, now that the worst had happened and he had lost his dream for good and all. I'm sure he blamed the whole thing on Agnes and was a little proud to be haunted as no man had ever been haunted before.

chapter seven

THE woods bosses still felt pressed for time to fill their orders and meet their quotas. Old Fox kept on hiring new men. By the first of August, we had seventy-five bursting into the cookhouse night and morning with their incredible appetites and still more to come. When the work became absolutely impossible, Old Fox brought us two new flunkeys, Midge and Bonny.

The two were sisters, fresh off a farm near Sumner and aquiver with delight at sight of all the stalwart young loggers pulled up to the tables, row after row. I have seen the same look in the eyes of ardent fishermen as they came upon a shaded bend in the Rogue and saw the steelhead leaping in the sunset light. Oh no! Not again! I thought morosely. What's the matter with Old Fox? Wouldn't you think—

Everybody in camp reacted in one way or another. After a look at the sexy, vulnerable sisters, old timers shook their heads, recognizing trouble wrapped up in those shapely packages. John Paul, anxious, no doubt, not to set Agnes off again, instantly took cover, confining himself to dish washing which allowed him to turn his back on Midge and Bonny the greater part of the time. But among the new young loggers who had not yet learned to amuse themselves with poker, mating rivalry built up rapidly.

The sisters were remarkably alike, both brown haired

and brown eyed, both with the same irrepressible giggle. Meatball kept the two busy all day with almost a sack of spuds to peel each morning and all the other vegetables to prepare. Still they had plenty of vigor left. At every opportunity, they flaunted their availability with roguish, eager eyes, and the chase was on.

Sometimes I wondered if I myself might not be growing a little too responsible and serious minded. Here were all these men and instead of frisking around like the sisters, I kept on frantically baking pies. Respectful admiration is a fine thing. But being chased through the woods might have its good points, too. I mean if they didn't actually catch you.

We had a hundred men in camp by that time. How can you frisk with a hundred men sitting at table, looking hungry and expectant? Each new face I saw meant more pies, more biscuits, and heaven help me, more hot cakes. Cooking for a hundred men is unbelievably more difficult than cooking for sixty or seventy. The kettles grew heavier and the problem of keeping food hot more troublesome. We were always having visitors, too: salesmen; truck delivery men who brought gas, oil and logging equipment; occasionally a stray fisherman or hunter. All comers were invited to stay and eat and no one refused. To me it was perfectly apparent that these men arranged quite deliberately to happen in at mealtime.

To add to the general confusion, among the new men was a hard core of pranksters. Sometimes during the morning rush, when the men were packing their lunches and the flunkeys were busy with the refills, one of these jokers would choose a victim and fill his white cup with milk. Since the mugs were always placed upside down on the plates, when the victim sat down to breakfast, from long habit he would automatically turn his cup over, thereby splashing half the table. Everybody within watching distance would roar with laughter at the silly expression on the victim's face. But it was the poor flunkey who had to clean up the mess. Even the girls, who admired practically everything the loggers did, grew annoyed at this particular piece of horseplay.

Matters took a more serious turn when they picked on Meatball. You'd think a first-class cook like Meatball would be treated with reverence, particularly since he was a kindly man, quite unlike so many cooks whose dispositions deteriorate with every hour spent standing over a hot stove and every ounce of fire water they take on. The men probably laid for Meatball because his paperback love stories struck them as funny. Loggers thoroughly approve of love. They just can't imagine *reading* about it.

In addition to the usual tricks, such as hanging a bucket of water over his doorway to tip and drench him when he came in, they took to grabbing the romance out of his hip pocket whenever they came within reaching distance. "Don't pay any attention to them," I said, trying to be consoling. "It's just some of these new punks. They think they're being funny."

But Meatball was a man of dignity and something happened one night which no man of dignity could stand. A young choker setter started reading aloud from one of the romances to a crowd of loudly guffawing loggers in the cookhouse. To make it particularly outrageous, he substituted Meatball's name for that of the hero, resulting in something like this: "For a long moment, Meatball stared down at his fallen foe before sheathing his sword and turning to find the Lady Matilda cowering against the battlements. Their glances locked and Meatball's pale, handsome face grew yet paler. 'Meatball, Meatball,' the Lady Matilda moaned and then she was in his arms and he was showering her face with kisses, seeking and finding her eager lips—"

When I saw Meatball's face I could have cried. That time they had caught him on the raw. Meatball blew his top. He jerked off his apron and threw it on the floor. "You can all go to hell," he yelled, rushing out of the cookhouse, followed by a tremendous belly laugh from the loggers.

I ran after him with Midge and Bonny at my heels and overtook him at the door of his cabin. Meatball was in a fearful state. He said he would never cook another mouthful for any of those bastards. We cajoled and pleaded but to no avail. He said if he even saw a logger again he was going to kick his teeth in. He said he didn't give a damn for the week's pay due him. He was going to get out and to hell with the whole camp. Then he went into his cabin and closed the door. We could hear him hauling valises out from under his bed and throwing shoes around.

In a few minutes Camp Push hurried over, but apparently he got no further than we did. When he came out again he shrugged his shoulders and walked off.

After Midge and Bonny had gone back to the cookhouse, I knocked timidly on Meatball's door. No answer. I knocked louder. Still no answer. A man who has been humiliated does not want sympathy, but I simply could not let that nice fat cook leave camp feeling as if he had no friends. I waited until he had finally loaded his car and climbed in, and then I ran over and poked my head through the window.

"I think you are the kindest, sweetest cook who ever lived," I said. I remembered how he had helped me when I first arrived, pretending not to notice when my pumpkin pies were scorched around the edges and taking as much of the work as he could on himself during Hoot Owl and

I grew a little tearful. "There will never be another cook like you," I said, wiping my eyes on my apron.

Meatball's face got red and he looked horribly shy. All of a sudden he glanced up with a wild look in his eyes. "I don't suppose there's any chance—oh, no. Ha! Ha! That's impossible, of course," he said. There was a long, pregnant pause. "Isn't it?" he added in a faint voice.

I must have looked stunned.

"No, no, of course not. Ha! Ha! Think nothing of it," he said, breathing loudly. He started his car, stalled the engine and worked feverishly for a minute before he got it rolling. But after he had gone a few yards, he stopped and reversed suddenly.

Oh dear, I thought, he's going to have another go at it. But no. The cook had come to the fore again.

"You'll find five legs of pork in the small walk-in," he said earnestly. "They're all scored and seasoned and there's applesauce in that white enameled pitcher. Good luck, my dear." And off he went, waving gallantly back at me, while I blew kisses until he disappeared across the bridge.

"Well," Camp Push said at my shoulder, "Old Fox will try to get a cook out here as soon as he can, Lee. But in the meantime, you'll have to get breakfast on as best you can, with John Paul and the girls."

"Me!" I yelped to Camp Push's retreating back. Well, of course there wasn't anybody except me to do it. But good heavens! A hundred men! I had bossed the cookhouse during Meatball's days off, but always on weekends when very few men were in camp.

I hardly slept a wink that night. Soft-boiled eggs, I thought. They're the easiest. But even with soft-boiled eggs, even with Midge to keep testing them and Bonny to watch the toast, breakfast was fifteen minutes late, while the loggers stood around the lunchroom door, ostentatiously tightening their belts to show how hungry they were. And you don't deserve *any* breakfast, I thought, remembering nice, kind Meatball.

I managed to get the bosses' noon dinner on the table. At four in the afternoon, five legs of fresh pork were almost done in the oven and I had just finished making cookies, when Old Fox arrived with the new cook.

"This is Peter Sims, Lee," he said.

The dark-eyed, bald-headed, wizened runt looked me over superciliously. "You may call me *Mister* Sims, Lee," he told me in precise tones.

"Lee will be glad to show you where things are," Old Fox said and fled.

Mr. Sims immediately proceeded to scald me. "Hey! What are you doing?" he barked. He jumped over to the kettle sink where I was working and made a grab at the hot-water hose we used for rinsing. As a result, the steaming jet spurted over my left foot. I grabbed at the foot in anguish, the worst thing I could have done. The hot anklet held the heat in and I began to bawl.

"Take your sock off, you young fool," Mr. Sims shouted, struggling to get the hose under control.

I spent the rest of the day in bed, salve smeared on my foot, reading one of Meatball's discarded paperbacks. When Midge brought my supper over, it turned out to be hash. "What happened to the roast pork?" I asked.

Midge was round eyed. "I think he fed them to the pigs. He took the roast beef you had for tomorrow's lunch table and made hash, along with fried potatoes and macaroni and cheese. And you ought to have heard the men muttering when they left the dining room."

This was my first experience with a peculiarity of professional cooks. They won't be caught dead serving anything another cook has prepared. Standing rib roasts, ham, turkey—into the garbage can they go whenever a new cook takes over. They could be models of culinary excellence. It makes no difference. The new cook looks at them with curled lip and heaves them out the door.

I was able to report for work the next morning, wearing a house slipper with the instep cut out. Mr. Sims asked me no questions about my injury. He served oatmeal mush and burnt toast for breakfast. Old Fox, thoroughly alarmed, took him into the office immediately after the meal and when Mr. Sims came out he was almost affable, although his eyes made me think of a trapped skunk's.

"You can tend to pastry, Lee," he said, and set Midge and Bonny to squeezing a whole crate of lemons. He himself started cutting up meat for supper. By the time my pies were ready to bake, every oven was full of meat scraps and bones.

"How can I bake my pies?" I finally asked.

"Your pies can wait until I've tried out that grease. Pies! Any good restaurant chef will tell you the entree is the only important thing in a meal."

"But the lunch tables," I began and then stopped. He had gone back to his meat cutting. It was almost suppertime before I got the pies baked. The men had to go without cookies. Pretty soon we were wading in bones and trimmings up to our ankles.

"There's no use even trying to sweep," Bonny wailed. "And this morning he told us to leave off the jam and the canned fruit and the men bawled *me* out."

"Cheer up," I said. "He won't last long. Just wait and see."

For the next few days, in spite of Mr. Sims, work in the

cookhouse limped along without interruption, except for the hysterical giggles of Midge and Bonny. As far as Bonny was concerned, I discovered which way the emotional winds were blowing as the result of a disastrous morning, a Saturday when the cookhouse crew all had to stay in camp because the men were still working half a day.

Since we expected a large contingent from the State Fire Patrol for the midday meal, I had come into the cookhouse early to start the light bread. The dough was set and I was grating hashbrowns for breakfast when Bonny and Midge arrived yawning widely. They took their coffee cups to a window and were standing there, drinking it and looking out when Midge yelled, "My God! Fire!" and ran out of the back door. We all followed.

Smoke spiraled out of the sheethouse halfway along the row of bunkhouses. A tongue of flame had already caught a wall of the shack adjoining it and a naked man was whaling the ground with a pair of burning pants, yelling, "FIRE! FIRE! HELP! Snoozy's in the sheethouse."

We all ran screaming toward the blaze. I heard John Paul shout, "Somebody get me a blanket. I'll go in after him."

"Wait, you idiots," Indian Johnny bellowed, running up with a rope. He tied one end around his waist and thrust the other end at John Paul. "If I yell 'pull,' you drag us out," he ordered and darted straight into the smoking sheethouse.

Half-dressed men poured from bunkhouses. Suddenly, the burning building exploded as a wedge of fire blew the ends off. In an instant the outline of the sheethouse was hidden by leaping flames. Midge and Bonny and I were all screaming, our voices lost in the general bedlam, the shouts of men, the pistol whip of crackling flames and the sound of breaking glass.

Indian Johnny could only have been gone a few seconds, but it seemed an endless nightmare before we heard his roar. John Paul pulled the rope gently to guide him and he stumbled out, bent almost double, his clothes on fire. In his arms was Snoozy, wrapped in the old tarp which he had been sleeping under, drunk as a hoot owl.

As soon as Indian Johnny set him down, Snoozy looked around, his eyes popped at the flames and he yelled, "Whoopie!"

Men tore at Indian Johnny's clothes. John Paul threw Snoozy's tarp around the reeling man and we led him to the cookhouse. Midge ran for the cooking brandy while I covered his blistered hands and arms with burn salve and wrapped them in clean dishtowels.

The loggers had been too intent watching Indian Johnny rescue Snoozy to remember the emergency pump on the river. When they finally started after it they found it was missing, taken to town by the camp Fire Warden for repairs. Men began crowding into the cookhouse, calling for buckets, boilers, kettles, anything that would hold water. Within two minutes, not even a big pitcher was left there.

The fire spread fast. Three bunkhouses were already ablaze. Swivelneck, his face blank with dismay, was wetting down the commissary walls with a water hose which would have been ineffectual against the burning bunkhouses. Men staggered up from the river, some under the burden of a huge boiler, others unaware how funny they looked running back and forth with a two-quart pitcher.

The heat was unbearable. Five more cabins were doomed and tongues of fire licked at the commissary walls. If that went, the cookhouse would be next. Drowning out the tumult of crackling flames and shouting men, I heard a new sound, a sudden great rattle and bang as a loose-jointed Cat clattered up with Wild Bill in the saddle. He had a wet wool shirt tied around his head and face. As the men saw what he was up to, they all froze still. The only sounds were the thunderous clang of the Cat, the roar of its motor and the hiss of flames biting into the bunkhouses.

Wild Bill lowered the blade of the Cat and charged directly toward the cabin nearest the commissary. For a moment he almost disappeared from sight as the Cat nudged against the burning walls, the flames enveloping him in a sort of infernal halo. The next moment he backed out again. Methodically charging forward, backing up, now in sight, now lost to view, he shoved all the burning buildings into one huge bonfire.

"Oh, he's wonderful, he's wonderful, he's wonderful," Bonny stammered. "Oh, he's wonderful—"

"He's quite a hunk of man," I admitted.

The sharp cleats on the Cat's track had cut through the buried water pipe. Swivelneck was trying to direct the leakage toward the commissary wall by holding up a board as a trough. With all the boilers, the kettles and the pitchers of water concentrated against the commissary, the fire eventually burned itself out.

Suddenly I remembered breakfast. "Somebody turn that electricity back on right this minute," I gasped. "We haven't even started breakfast."

Moonshine Jake winked at Bonny. "As soon as the fire makes any coals, this gal puts the grill over them and starts frying hot cakes."

Bonny did not even hear him. She was gazing mesmerized at Wild Bill—the very last person a susceptible little kid like Bonny ought to be gazing at. They simply weren't in the same league. "Come on," I said. "They'll all be hungry as bears."

When breakfast was finally ready, Bonny placed a platter of fried eggs in front of Wild Bill as reverently as if she were ministering to a god.

Most of the men had lost everything they owned in the fire except for the clothes they had hurriedly dived into. The commissary shelves grew bare, Swivelneck gloating over every sale, until Old Fox caught him hiking prices. "It's just a question of merchandising," I overheard Swivelneck saying defensively. "Supply and demand. When anything is in short supply, the price goes up."

"Not around here it doesn't," Old Fox growled, looking exactly like an incensed bull, his short grey hair growing low on his forehead, his stocky legs planted belligerently apart.

Fortunately the new dormitory was almost ready, although only about half the rooms were completely finished. When Snoozy sobered up, it took all his tact and wheedling to placate loggers assigned to half-finished rooms.

The first chance I had, I took a look at our bottle of vanilla extract. Sure enough, it was almost gone. Snoozy must have guzzled a pint, probably in the middle of the night, and then headed for the sheethouse to sleep it off as was his custom when he had a bun on. I have no doubt his lighted cigar had fallen on a pile of cleaning rags. He would have done better to stick to snoose. From that time on I tried to keep the vanilla extract hidden. Not that it would do much good, I suspected. Snoozy had a nose like a truffle hound for smelling out anything with an alcoholic content.

The summer days stayed hot and the work kept up at a roaring pace. Sometimes the truck drivers would not get in until nine thirty or ten. To me, weekends off were the only calm moments in a hurry-scurry nightmare. Like the loggers, I stopped counting time by days. I would think "five sleeps" or "six sleeps" before I can get to town. The days were a blur of dough, sizzling heat and hungry mouths to feed.

One weekend I was too tired even to go to town. I decided instead to stay in camp and rest—that is, until I bumped into Edison Smith on Sunday morning.

"I should think you'd be sick of camp," he said. "How about going for a picnic with Wild Bill and me in the Louse?"

"Fun," I told him, lingering there and wondering if this nice quiet man really was crazy for me, the way Gina had said. I had never tried to flirt with Edison, thinking it would be a little like flirting with Abraham Lincoln. Still, there could be no harm in trying. I took a leaf from Midge and Bonny's book, the swift upward glance, the swing to the hips. Right away he stopped looking like Abraham Lincoln. No doubt about it, there was a very decided gleam in his eyes and fun in the grin he gave me. I approved of this. It showed a proper orientation toward life.

As we rattled past the cookhouse in the miniature crummy, I spotted Bonny and Midge standing on the porch, open mouthed to see me sailing off in such noble company. Bonny would have given her all to be driving away with Wild Bill. She would have been happy to crawl up the road behind him.

Even though the Louse was a noisy wench and jounced roughly over the narrow, dusty road, my spirits soared as soon as we were away from the uproar of camp life. Once a herd of about forty elk raced along in front of us, the white aprons on their backsides winking in the sunlight.

They all looked to me like second cooks with their aprons in the wrong places.

When Wild Bill stopped the Louse, we followed a well-marked deer trail through the grass to the far end of a forest glade. There was no sign of logging there. Huge firs surrounded the natural clearing, so still and lovely a place that I felt I ought to walk softly not to break into its peace. Once more I was surprised at the absence of bird life. There was not a single twitter or flutter of a wing.

Edison said the only small birds they ever saw in those deep woods were a few camp robbers—Canadian jays—who hung around like little beggars while the men were eating lunch.

I could not walk very quietly and yet keep up with the long strides of the two woodsmen. I found myself breaking into a half trot and taking a skipping step every few feet until we finally stopped beside a forest pool. The pool, I realized at once, was a surprise Edison had been storing up for me. "Well, here you are," he said, presenting the pool exactly as if it were a bouquet. If he had dug it with his bare hands, he could not have looked prouder. And no wonder. It was as clear as a mirror, almost round and surrounded by rocks where sedums and maidenhair fern grew. A tin cup stood on a rock beside it. When Edison had rinsed it well he dipped up some water for me to drink, water as cold as ice and with a sparkle to it.

We settled down to our lunch by the poolside and I felt exactly like Eve out there in an unspoiled Eden with two Adams. I glanced at Wild Bill and corrected myself. Wild Bill did not fit into the Adam picture. Edison now, he would be a splendid Adam. I smiled at him fondly, which seemed to surprise and delight him no end. But Wild Bill—no, not

Adam. He was no snake certainly, but he might pass as the Devil in some far more attractive disguise.

Unfortunately at the end of a wonderfully happy picnic, my ego took a beating. I remembered the cup sitting by the poolside and exclaimed, "Why, the works must be near here. The men have been using that cup to drink from."

"Just beyond those trees," Wild Bill said.

I had never seen the works nor a rigged sparpole, but when I urged them to take me there, Edison and Wild Bill exchanged a peculiar glance. "I guess we'd better get back to camp," Edison said.

"Oh well, why not have a look?" Wild Bill said. There was a humorous glint in his eyes as I jumped up and we started off.

"The men have too much time on their hands these days," he said. "Guys sleeping all over the woods. Don't know what Old Fox is thinking of." He shook his head solemnly and turned his head to look at Edison.

"Yes, so I've heard. Camp Push told me they didn't get out a foot more this month than last. He about goes nuts trying to get work out of all these new punks."

"He fired seven last week."

"Old Fox must have hired seven more," I said. "All twelve tables are full with a man at each end, too."

When we reached the works, in every direction I saw broken saplings, silvery stumps and logs lying apparently helter-skelter with the donkey engine, looking forsaken, crouched among them waiting for the morrow. The sparpole towered above the machinery. It was a tall, straight tree, topped and stripped of its branches, with guylines, like the bare ribs of a half-opened umbrella, fastened to a ring of stumps surrounding it. A cable reached from what they called the "bull block" at the top of the sparpole to the donkey.

Edison explained that the cable, with the help of the donkey, yarded the logs into a pile known as the cold deck. From there the logs were loaded onto trucks with a loading bitch. The loading bitch, I learned, was a strange-looking contraption which could swing around, pick up a log and drop it onto a waiting truck.

He was saying something about two logs fastened to a short sparpole, but I lost the sequence. Two strange-looking stumps caught my eye.

"What are those?"

"Oh nothing," Edison said. "We'd better start back."

I peered at the stumps. Then I marched over. Some logger, expert with his ax, had carved torsos out of them. Shades of Mae West! Even she would have looked flat chested beside those stumps. At the base of one, "Bonny" was written in green chalk. Under the other, "Midge."

I looked furtively around. No, there was no carved stump inscribed "Lee." I couldn't for the life of me understand why the artist had failed to notice my qualifications. An omission of the kind can make a person feel extremely deflated. Not that I was going to let Edison and Wild Bill see my chagrin. "Hm, very expert work," I said critically. "I'm surprised, too. I've heard some tales about loggers and their axes—trying to hang doors with them and splitting them right down the middle and—"

"What malarkey!" Edison remonstrated. "You know darn well we shave with them."

As we drove back to camp, I looked curiously at Wild Bill. "Bonny has been practically knocking herself out, trying to get you to look at her. If you don't pay her some mind pretty soon, she's liable to pour soup down your neck, just so you'll know she's alive."

Wild Bill chuckled. "I'm not getting into that rat race. How old are the kids anyway? Seventeen?"

"Midge is twenty and Bonny eighteen."

"Over the age of consent, at least," Wild Bill said. "Say, Ed, did you see Bob Botts' black eye this morning?"

"Sure did. And Reese Downey's split knuckles, too."

I knew tension among the raunchy young loggers chasing Midge and Bonny had continued to mount as the sisters flipped their skirts around the dining room, but this was the first time I realized that actual fights had developed. Bob Botts was the husky donkey puncher who had lost over $300 to Al King at poker. Reese Downey was a red-headed high climber, better known as Reese-the-Rig. Midge had been going for rides or strolls with one or the other of them almost every evening.

As far as I could tell, that night at supper, things were peaceful enough though, at the moment, and within a few days, Bob Botts' eye faded to a bilious pink and Reese's hand seemed normal again.

One evening Snoozy was playing his harmonica in the cookhouse and the rest of the gang had gathered around harmonizing. On such occasions, some lonesome logger who wanted to talk invariably cornered me. This evening it was Moonshine Jake. I had already heard the story of how he joined the I.W.W. as a kid in Idaho, but I liked Jake, his weather-beaten wrinkles, his stoop, his skinny cordlike frame and all, so I did not mind hearing the tale again. It centered around a hobo camp he had stumbled onto down by the railroad tracks while he was looking for strays from his father's ranch. The I.W.W. was getting into its swing then and the stories he heard in that hobo camp fired Jake's imagination and gave him a cause.

"There was always a big pot of stew hanging from an iron trivet over the campfire. On a cool still night I'd smell it a long way before I got there. I kinda guessed the basic ingredients came from my father's herd, but it didn't bother me. My God—the songs they'd sing. Better than a revival, gal. There was something big going on all around the country. It wasn't like these namby-pamby union meetings we have now. After any big I.W.W. gathering we'd always ask 'Anybody killed? How many hurt?'

"It was all fine until some damn fools killed the Governor and then we all lit out. I headed north with my pony, a bed roll and a few measly dollars."

I was too busy hearing about his first job in a logging camp up in the Canadian woods to notice Bob Botts and Reese-the-Rig by the dining-room door until all at once I heard Bob roar, "Try and make me, you pink-haired punk!" Then there was a big SPLATT!

Jake's mouth stayed open like a constipated fish and Snoozy's harmonica died a-squeaking. We all jumped up. Bob Botts and Reese Downey were slugging it out, toe to toe.

"Get out of my kitchen," Mr. Sims screamed, pushing through the crowd with the meat cleaver. "Out! All of you *out!*" He shoved between the two and before they could pull their punches, a blow landed alongside his head from each of them. Mr. Sims staggered, recovered and slashed out wildly with the meat cleaver, shouting swear words while the men all moved back and escaped out of the front door. Mr. Sims shut and locked the door, glowered at me, Bonny and Midge and then went out the back door himself.

The last thing we intended was to stay sequestered in

the cookhouse. We drew back the bolt, scuttled out and huddled together like three frightened heifers on the front porch. The yard was in turmoil. Men had come running from every direction. I was glad to see Indian Johnny holding Bob Botts and Wild Bill and Edison holding Reese-the-Rig.

"I'm glad somebody has some sense," I said and then stared, unbelieving. The men were not trying to stop the fight. They were simply hanging onto Bob and Reese while the other men laid their bets.

"Simmer down, you young fools," Snoozy said reasonably. "You've got plenty of time." He had a pad and pencil and was circulating through the crowd, scribbling furiously, followed by Moonshine who gathered in the money.

Most of the loggers wanted to put money on Reese-the-Rig, so the odds reached five to one. Bob Botts's only backers seemed to be his donkey crew and Swivelneck. By that time the entire camp surrounded the combatants and I saw Camp Push running toward the crowd, fastening up his pants as he ran.

"He'll put a stop to this nonsense," I said with relief. Instead he hurried over to the commissary and turned the yard lights on so the scene came out in glaring relief. As he later took pains to explain to me, when a deplorable tension builds up, in spite of their efforts to prevent it, nothing clears the air like a good tough fight.

Snoozy finally had all the bets written down and they turned the fighters loose. The two seemed evenly matched to me, judging by the regular and emphatic exchange of blows. Every time Reese-the-Rig rocked Bob Botts back on his heels, Midge pounded a fist against her open hand with noisy glee. It seemed to me that even if Bob Botts won the fight, he had already lost the battle.

Then I saw that Reese-the-Rig was in trouble, running a hand across his eyes every few seconds.

"My God!" Midge cried and we had all we could do to hold her there.

It was a ridiculous sight, two young men beating each other's brains out, surrounded by a yelling, screaming, groaning, cheering ring of men. So why on earth, I thought, shocked, do I have such a feeling of unbearable excitement and why am I tingling all over with a delicious pleasure?

Reese-the-Rig got in an extra powerful punch to Bob Botts's midriff and Bob fell over backwards. Catlike, he turned over on all fours, grabbed up a wicked-looking stick from the ground and banged Reese Downey over the head with it.

The crowd stiffened—all but Midge, who rushed out screaming and held Reese-the-Rig's head in her lap. Then Indian Johnny stepped up, his big stooped shoulders swaying a little from side to side, and knocked Bob Botts cold with one blow. "All bets are off," he said. "Moonshine and and Snoozy'll give you back your money."

"And," Wild Bill roared out, "if any of you jerks tell the Rig who knocked Bob Botts out, he'll get the same from me."

When Reese-the-Rig came to, he looked around and said, "Jumping catfish. I must have got in a lucky punch." I don't think he ever learned differently.

Old Fox and Camp Push had a conference the next morning. That afternoon Old Fox paid a visit to the young sirens in their cabin. Whatever he said to them proved to be extremely effective. After that, the two were the most demure young women I ever saw. No more swinging hips. Even their bosoms seemed remarkably deflated all at once.

Well, for heaven's sake, I thought. Falsies. The little

scamps. Both of them perfectly adequately endowed by nature, too. I rather suspected the stump carver would feel his art had been betrayed. There were still a lot of irrepressible giggles and an air of intrigue, but the fights, at least, stopped.

chapter eight

❧ I WAS right about Mr. Sims. He did not last long. In less than two weeks he slipped the men a mess of tainted hamburger. A lucky thing it was, too, that the loggers had moved into their new dormitory with a bath between every two rooms. For several days the camp was made up of nothing but green apple two-steppers.

During the worst of the scourge I was helping Midge and Bonny reset the tables after supper when Moonshine Jake sauntered past us and said out of the corner of his mouth, "There's a meeting tonight."

If an unannounced union meeting is held in a logging camp, the cook might as well start packing immediately. Generally he is alerted by the grapevine and takes off in a flurry of dust and hastily packed suitcases before the meeting begins. Nobody felt inclined to alert Mr. Sims. He retired complacently to his couch and before long the loggers began drifting back to the cookhouse. John Paul, Midge, Bonny and I were all union members, but we took seats well in the back of the dining room, trying to be as inconspicuous as possible since the meeting involved our department.

The union steward called the meeting to order. "We'll get right down to the business in hand," he said, "before anyone has to make a run for it."

This quip was met with thunderous laughter and two men leaped up and made a dash for the door.

Moonshine Jake immediately demanded the floor, the old crusading fire ablaze in his eyes. "Arise ye prisoners of starvation," he thundered. "Arise, ye wretched of the earth."

All of us prisoners of starvation applauded wildly and Jake blasted right off into a ringtailed roarer of a speech. It was impossible to make out who was being blamed for Mr. Sims and the tainted hamburgers. It seemed to be either the lumber barons and the "whole rotten system" or else the commies who had busted up the I.W.W. (according to Jake). Anyway, it was a very stirring address and everybody stamped and cheered. This so encouraged Jake that he broke into song, one having to do with a fast freight and his friends in the jungle. There was a good deal in it about mulligan stew and the life of a hobo.

"Hear, hear!" the crowd echoed.

The shop steward rapped for order. "Sit down, Jake. This is a meeting, not a sideshow."

Jake sat, unsubdued, and someone shouted, "Go out in the jungles and bring back a jug, Moonshine."

Again the steward rapped for order. "The chair is still waiting to entertain a motion," he said.

Snoozy jumped up. "Let's hang him," he said.

"Sit down!" the steward bellowed. "Do you want to get this done or don't you? A lot of these men are very uncomfortable. If somebody will make a motion, maybe they can get back to the can."

When the laughter had subsided a young logger got up very solemnly and made a motion that Mr. Sims be asked to leave at once. The motion was seconded, passed by unanimous vote, a committee was named to break the news to Mr. Sims in the morning and the meeting hurriedly adjourned.

Ornery as he was I still felt sorry for Mr. Sims. He

seemed such a friendless little man. I was almost relieved when, in the end, he was not fired after all. He must have heard the hubbub in the dining room and guessed its meaning. When I came into the cookhouse the next morning, I found he had filled three forty-gallon garbage cans with "leftovers" and taken off down the river.

After breakfast, which we got onto the table as best we could, we all pitched in to clean up the place. John Paul lugged in another big garbage can, put it between the two walk-ins and we filled that, too, with spoiling meat.

During Mr. Sims's term of office, Swivelneck had done very little snooping around the cookhouse, put off, no doubt, by the sight of the cook eternally sharpening his knives which he explained were "to trim noses that were too long." After Mr. Sims disappeared, however, Swivelneck lost no time in looking things over. He stood watching us as we continued to pile smelly meat into the can, not saying a word, but with his face as pained at sight of the waste as if it had all been trimmed off his own skinny bones.

There followed a period known as the Parade of the Cooks—erstwhile short-order cooks, dinner cooks, slumgullion throwers, chefs. All of them hit the road after a few days. Either the work was too hard, the weather too hot or they were too thirsty. After each hurried departure the kitchen crew would be stuck cleaning up the mess he left behind, and I would have to leap panic stricken into the breach, responsible for the whole cookhouse, urging on the girls and John Paul, trying desperately to keep the loggers well fed. My status bounced around as fast as the cooks did. One day the kitchen crew would be kowtowing and the next day, when a new cook arrived, I would be one of the gang again.

A good-natured cook called Frisco, popular in the kitchen

because he did not work us too hard, had to leave precipitately when a logger caught him wiping his nose on his apron. "And that ties it," Old Fox said. "Lee, you are now first cook, whether you like it or not."

"Oh no, Boss, not me," I begged. "Please have a heart. I can't do it. Those pans are too heavy. I don't know enough. I'll never get the right amount cooked."

"Nonsense, gal, you've been here for months." He looked very solemn and said, "The whole camp has grown to depend on you, Lee."

This was an absolutely astonishing thought—a hundred men all depending on me, on the problem member of the family, who couldn't hold down a job and never made wise, sensible decisions! "Well, I'll be damned," I said. I had not looked seriously at my thumbs for a month. There had been no need for reassurance. But I hurriedly examined them now. They looked more competent than ever, capable of feeding a thousand men.

Old Fox was quite a psychologist in his way. "Don't think I haven't noticed how you've kept things rolling when a cook has been drunk or just plain goofing off. As I said to Push, 'There's a gal with a head on her shoulders and a heart of gold.'"

"That's what you told Camp Push?" I asked weakly.

Old Fox nodded. "I sure did. I said, 'It was a lucky day for the Ticoma when Lee walked into the office. Would you believe it,' I said, 'a pretty little blonde like that? And here she's kept the whole camp on its feet.'"

"We-ell," I murmured, stunned. "But only for a few weeks, Boss. Just until some qualified man comes along. And I will have to have more help."

"Of course you will." Old Fox made a magnanimous gesture toward the dining room. "Pick out anybody you want from that bunch of greenhorns I hired last week. Gad, some of them don't know a stump from their own hind ends."

During a lull in the kitchen while the men were finishing supper I took a good look at Old Fox's greenhorns. They were not hard to recognize. Some of them were even talking at table, a thing no real logger would dream of doing. One blond youth of about twenty was extra clean and alert looking. He was husky and I thought he might be intelligent.

"Who is that in place three on table eight?" I asked Bonny, feeling sure she would know the name of such a handsome boy.

"That boy over there? Wow! What a doll! That's Kevin Kales."

After supper, Old Fox said I certainly could have Kevin Kales if I thought I could teach him anything. "I don't know why these college boys keep trying to be loggers during the summer. That one's a likeable kid but he's leery of the woods."

Kevin was delighted to be away from them and in the cookhouse he proved quite useful. I even taught him to make golden, flaky pies. I suspect his baking-powder biscuits were better than mine.

So there I was, heading a crew of five and subject to the most hideous nightmares whenever I went to sleep. During the daytime the kitchen ran smoothly. The flunkeys and Kevin enjoyed working together and John Paul kept the place shining. But as soon as I went to sleep at night the horrible dreams began. I would see the loggers racing for the supper table (only in my dream there appeared to be a thousand) and I would have only one small ham to feed them all. I would begin frantically trying to broil pork chops to piece out with, but the chops would not broil and besides, would just five pork chops feed such a crowd? I would wake up, sick with fright, groan with relief at discovering it was all a dream and go back to sleep again, only to find myself at a loggers' meeting with Moonshine Jake roaring out: "The men have lost fifty-seven pounds apiece. Now they're so weak they can't walk. We have to carry them."

During my waking hours, planning menus and making out the orders were the biggest headaches. The job took up most of the afternoon. No more lovely swims in the river. Swivelneck went after supplies three times a week and he insisted on going over my lists item by item while I fought every inch of the way. Since I was neither of the physique nor temperament to take after him with a meat cleaver, he felt safe in throwing his weight around, poking his nose in everything like a hound smelling out a trail.

On the surface, I remained composed enough. "One large log lost down a canyon is worth more than I can waste in a month," I learned to snap back.

Once, instead of the choice steer quarters we were accustomed to, he brought utility cow, so tough I could not even dent the tenderloin. It was marked "choice" steer on the invoice, too, I discovered, and had cost accordingly. Another time, after hearing Snoozy speak nostalgically of creamed codfish and new potatoes, I told Swivelneck to change the order of oysters for Friday's supper to codfish. I also urged him to make sure the codfish was boned and of first grade. I expected Swivelneck to be pleased at my economy. Instead, when I prepared to soak the codfish Thursday night, I found it was not only yellow and smelly, it was also chock full of bones. That time I simply picked up the whole mess and put it in the front seat of Swivelneck's car, knowing he would find it with a vengeance when he went home on Saturday at noon.

Swivelneck never mentioned the codfish to me, but very soon he complained about the lunch table. "The men can't possibly pack away all the junk you have the girls put on," he said. "I was shocked when I saw it this morning."

I suspected he had never watched Powder Box Pete loading his lunch. I had watched Pete for months and still I could not believe my eyes, although Edison had explained the phenomenon. He said Pete was a jackhammer man, able to place his powder-box dinner pail in a strategic place and dip into it all day long. As far as I could see, he never gained an ounce, either. His string-bean body was emaciated and his eyes never lost their hungry look.

After a little urging, Swivelneck agreed to come early to the cookhouse and watch the procedure. I had breakfast well under way by the time he arrived, looking sleepy and grouchy. I had also moved a few cans on a storeroom shelf to give us a peeking eye view into the lunchroom. The room was full of men stowing their lunches away in dinner pails. Before long I spotted Powder Box Pete among them, carrying his powder box.

"Now just wait," I whispered.

The box was too big to set on the shelves along each side of the room where the men kept their lunch buckets. Instead he put it down in a corner, glancing nervously at it every few minutes as if he expected someone to snatch out a tidbit at any moment. He had lined the almost bushel box with newspaper. Into this little nest, he dropped two loaves of bread and half a pound of butter wrapped in waxed paper. Then he filled a quart jar with canned peaches and a pint jar with tuna mix and put these in, too. After that he dropped a handful of lettuce leaves, rings of green peppers, a dozen or so onion slices and half a dozen large dill pickles into a paper sack.

Swivelneck let out a distressed sigh and I ducked away from our peephole. "No one's looking this way," he whispered so I came out again.

Powder Box Pete had spread out a strip of waxed paper on the lunch counter. Onto this he heaped a stack of cold meat higher than his greedy hand, a dozen slices of cheese and two hard fried eggs. Next he filled a sack with two handfuls of cookies and a piece of cake. The powder box was almost full, but he managed to crowd in an apple pie, three oranges and six bananas.

It was time for me to start frying the eggs and hot cakes, but as I hurried toward the stove a dazed Swivelneck made one of his rare human remarks. "Lee," he said, "you better have Kevin bake an extra couple of pies today. Powder Box Pete seems to be fixing to starve himself."

I remembered my dream of the starving loggers. Well, it was not the men who had been losing weight since I had taken over the cookhouse. It was me. Nearly a pound a day. I was getting bone tired. I had even started spilling and dropping things in the kitchen. Giving my all for good old Ticoma, I thought grimly. There I was, weighed down by responsibility, anxiously studying the faces of loggers to see if they were satisfied with the veal roasts; starting up out of a sound sleep, wondering if I had forgotten to order cinnamon or if the butter would hold out until Swivelneck went to town again; struggling endlessly with menus; my stomach tightening up with fright when the turkeys looked tough, asking myself if the loggers would stand still for a touch of garlic in the salad dressing, just to vary the flavor, or if that would be the straw to break the camel's back. And what on earth *for?* I asked myself indignantly.

Just to prove something to myself? I already had proved something. The cookhouse had run smoothly (greased with my sweat), the kitchen crew had stayed on their toes, and the meals had been good.

In my heart I knew why I was in there laboring like a donkey engine. It was because Old Fox had told me to and all my life I had been trying desperately to do what people expected of me, whether it was what I wanted or not. Well, I thought, it was time I woke up. To hell with it.

It was then exactly six thirty. Time for breakfast. I walked out onto the porch and beat the triangle. I had become fairly good with the triangle. I could make it sound like temple bells or an African tribal dance. This morning I added some loud fanfares of independence, a touch of the "Marseillaise" and even a suspicion of Moonshine's "Arise, ye prisoners of starvation."

All during breakfast I kept peering in at Old Fox, comfortably eating my hashbrowns and eggs and felt my dander rising. I waylaid him as he started out the door. "Look, my friend," I said, taking up a determined stance, "I have had it. I can't take this first cook's job any longer—"

"Nonsense, gal," Old Fox said, edging toward the door. "Everything's been going good. The meals are wonderful. Those mashed potatoes last night were fluffy as clouds. Like I said to Push—"

"No you don't," I cried out. "I'm nearly done in. And now Kevin will be going back to college next week—"

Old Fox immediately seized on this remark. "You'll need help. I can see that. Tell you what I'll do. I'll get you a good second cook...."

I began wringing my hands. "Please, please, Old Fox. Go down to that employment office and find a great big, strong, sober first cook."

"Well, I'll try," he grunted ungraciously and left.

He came back from town just as we had finished supper. I was in the storeroom slicing the breakfast bacon on the electric slicer when he walked in and sat down on the chopping block—a serious offense in a camp cookhouse. "He'sh here, gal," he yelled above the noise of the slicer. "Over to the cook'sh shack!"

"Thank heaven," I yelled back, too involved with the slicer at the moment to look at him. "When is he coming to take over this madhouse?"

"He'sh not. Unnerstand? He'sh a shecond cook."

I shut off the slicer. Old Fox was drunk as a goat. "What did you say?" I demanded.

"Shecond cook!" He glared at me. "I brought Lee a shecond cook!" He chuckled triumphantly.

"Did you bring me a shroud, too?" I did not even try to keep the bitterness out of my voice.

At that moment John Paul came into the storeroom. Old Fox grabbed him by the arm and led him out of the back door. I followed them to the porch, angrily watching Old Fox staggering down the steps, bowlegs and all.

Two hours later, with the evening work finally done, Midge, Bonny, Kevin and I sat wearily at the little table in the kitchen drinking coffee. The young high climber, Reese-the-Rig, had just joined us when the back door opened and Old Fox came in, keeping his balance with difficulty. He wove his way over to our table and with his countenance stern and dignified, pointed a finger at Kevin. "Yer fired," he bellowed. Then he pointed at Midge and Bonny. "Yer fired and yer fired." With precarious mincing steps, he turned and managed to make the back door, where he hung on a moment and then disappeared. We heard a big clatter as he fell off the porch.

"Gad, I wish he'd included me." I laughed.

The sisters both broke into tears and wailing.

"Oh, for heaven's sake, don't be silly," I told them. "Pay no attention to him. He's just overexhilarated, that's all. Pretend you didn't hear him."

"I'll take you girls to town," Reese-the-Rig offered.

"Oh no!" I protested. "He didn't mean it."

"Sure as hell sounded like he did." Reese had a huge, comforting paw on Midge's shoulder. "He can't talk to my fiancée that way." It was the first I had heard of any engagement.

Both girls brightened up considerably at the mention of town. Neither of them had been in for nearly two weeks.

"I'll take you all in my car," Kevin said. "It'll teach the old coot a lesson."

I pleaded and argued. It did no good. They all took off like a bunch of kids on a Hallowe'en spree, elated partly at the idea of getting even with Old Fox and partly at the prospect of an evening in town.

"We'll come back after our things next week," they shouted, scrambling into Kevin's car.

I sat down disconsolately, feeling left out and forsaken. My declaration of independence certainly had not come off. Instead of shelving my responsibilities, apparently I was going to struggle through breakfast with only John Paul and the new second cook to help. I had got around to hoping the second cook knew his business when Camp Push walked in.

"I bring tidings," he said and his voice sounded unhappy to me.

"You mean camp's shutting down tomorrow? I hope?"

Camp Push hunched up his big shoulders. "I hate to tell you this, Lee, but John Paul and the new second cook are out with Old Fox, all gloriously drunk. You'll have to get by with just Kevin and the girls in the morning. Can you do it?"

I started to laugh and I couldn't stop.

"Have you flipped?" Camp Push demanded.

After a few dry sobs I managed to choke off. "No," I gasped, "not yet, I don't think. But Old Fox has fired the girls and Kevin, too."

Camp Push looked as if I had kicked him in the teeth. "Oh, my God," he said. He had actually grown a little pale. "We can't shut down now. We can't even miss a day and still fill our orders. I'm in Dutch with the big shots already. What on earth can we do, Lee?"

I liked the sound of that "we" so much that I collected my scrambled wits and tried to think.

Camp Push brightened up a little. "Say, I've got a couple of young choker setters I could send over—"

"You could not! They'd just be in the way." I considered for a moment. "Well, maybe they could wash dishes at that."

"You mean," Push said in an awed voice, "you're going to get breakfast alone?"

"Cook it anyway." All at once I felt like Horatio at the bridge and sat up straighter. "I could borrow a page from all the drunken cooks we've had. We always have boiled eggs the morning after."

"Lee, you're a jewel." There was fervor in Push's voice. "You're a rare—"

"Hush now. I'm trying to think." The bacon was sliced. I could load the pans that night and grate the hashbrowns. There was also enough sliced bread for toast. The hot-cake batter would have to wait until morning, but the ingredients could be measured out that night. "I'll try it," I said. "But I couldn't possibly serve it."

Camp Push looked not only relieved, but also remarkably smug, now that he had passed the buck along. I studied him for a moment. "How about your getting here at five to set the cold stuff on and load the lunch table?" It was most effective. The smug look disappeared immediately. In fact, I have never seen a man more taken aback.

"We-ell," he stammered. "If you think I could help—"

"Then that's settled. We'll put the hot stuff on the serving counter and say, 'Boys, it's all yours. If you don't come and get it, Hans's pigs will.'"

"I don't know how I can ever pay you for getting me out of this spot," Push said.

By that time I was feeling very uppity. "The extra hundred last month when I'd cleaned up after the slumgullion specialist, didn't hurt my feelings a bit."

He grinned and started toward the door.

"Oh, Camp Push!" I called.

"Huh?"

"Stay sober."

He shut the door with an exaggerated caution, far more effective than slamming.

So I was a jewel. Nobody ever called a *really* important person a "jewel." People called a cook a jewel who turned out a good meal. Or a private secretary if she was discreet. But I had yet to hear the term used in connection with a chairman of the board at General Motors.

I had a hard time getting to sleep and when I did I kept waking every few minutes. At 3 A.M. I heard a car drive in and then a lot of giggles. I was still two-thirds asleep, but I pulled on a robe, switched on the light and stuck my head out of the door. Midge and Bonny were slipping by toward their cabin. Giggling sounds awfully silly when you are not doing it yourself. At the moment it made me feel a hundred years old, with my frisky youth a thing of the past.

"Well, where did *you* come from?" I asked.

"Hortense persuaded us to come back," Midge said, on the defensive at once.

"Mrs. Knowland, you know," Bonny put in.

"Of course I know. But how on earth did she find out?"

Midge shrugged. "Search me. She came down to Jug's Tavern looking for us. We'd only had one beer apiece, honest. Anyway, she said she'd fix that Casper and we'd better get back to camp that very moment. So here we are."

"You've only got two hours to sleep, so you'd better start in," I said, sounding just as crabby as I felt.

"Kevin isn't staying," Bonny called out as I started to close my door. "He's just picking up his things and going right back. His school starts next week—"

I didn't care what Kevin did. It would have been sort of fun to pull off the breakfast alone, I thought, as I went back to bed. I would have loved to boss Camp Push around for a few minutes. Now it was just anticlimax, hard work instead of drama.

With Bonny and Midge to help, breakfast was only a few minutes late. Old Fox, puny and pale, took his place at table and helped himself generously to the tomato juice which I told the flunkeys to put on. It is as much as a camp cook's job is worth to forget tomato juice Monday morning. This was not Monday, but we played it safe.

Anyone who has lived in a logging camp knows it is wisest not even to hold a thought he does not want shouted from the surrounding trees. By nine o'clock that morning, everybody knew how Hortense had found out about Old

Fox's spree. Snoozy, when sober, was like a reformed prostitute. He did not want anyone else to have any fun, either, so he had hiked up to the Fire Warden's cabin and, telling him there was a camp emergency, was allowed to use the fire-line radio. The warden almost had a stroke when he overheard Snoozy's "emergency." Nevertheless, headquarters phoned the boss's wife and Hortense was alerted.

Indian Johnny, who lived in the bunkhouse next to the bosses' shack, had heard the shower running most of the night, as well as groans, curses and howls of "but baby!" If we had not all been a little afraid of him, Old Fox would have turned into "But Baby" then and there. As it was, we kept a discreet silence and were careful not to let him intercept any amused glances.

He was morosely sipping his midmorning coffee at ten when Hortense appeared for breakfast, gayer and more flamboyant than ever, as if she had gathered strength from the exertions of the night. "You don't have to ask me," she shouted out when she saw me. "Sure, I'll bake the pies today." She let herself down on the bench beside Old Fox. "And when I get the pies baked we'll go down and send up a cook, won't we, Casper?"

"Yes, baby," Old Fox said meekly.

I heard afterward that Old Fox waited around the Employment Office all afternoon, using up three packages of cigarettes, lighting one and then another and throwing them away after a puff or two. But when he came back to camp after supper he had a cook in tow. My first sensation when I saw the new cook was dismay. He was past seventy, little and thin, with white hair in a fluffy halo around a bald spot on the top of his head. Arthritis had given him a permanent limp. Yet, in spite of these signs of senescence, his entrance into the cookhouse was sensational. On a leash he was leading a huge golden Persian kitten wearing a jeweled collar.

"Lee," Old Fox said, "this is Lucien."

Lucien made a courtly little bow. "Enchanted."

I looked into his face and saw that it was marked by many past griefs and disasters, but I also saw that he had the eye of command, and that is a comforting thing to find in a cookhouse. There was something more. The quality came right out to meet me. Lucien was a man of parts.

He had only cooked one meal when the entire camp settled back with a sense of relief. This time we had a *cook*. I have no idea whatever brought him to Coos Bay and thence to the Ticoma. In a logging camp you never ask questions about a person's past. But clearly, all his life, he had been used to the very finest kitchens. Sometimes I wondered if, by accident, he could have dumped arsenic instead of sugar into a soufflé, thereby antagonizing the clientele of some magnificent restaurant. Not that it worried me. I felt as if I had been struggling up a hill, laden down with fifty pounds of roast beef and five hundred oysters and had finally been able to let my burden drop.

chapter nine

❧ POSSIBLY, in his heart, Lucien hoped to make gourmets out of our loggers by easy stages. He was no fool—he kept pretty well to the good, hearty routine of steaks and roasts, all superbly cooked and perfectly seasoned. But every once in a while he could not resist slipping in something a little strange to the loggers, a mushroom here, a touch of saffron there.

Loggers are the most conservative of men when it comes to food. They simply do not care for exotic adventures in eating or new taste sensations. They appreciate good cooking; they can tell in a second if their beans are properly seasoned and the roast beef just rare enough. But try an unfamiliar flavor on them and they immediately become antagonistic. Generally the unaccustomed dishes would come back untouched or, above the usual table conversation of "Pass this," "Pass that," or "Short stop," we would hear someone say, "What's *that?*" in the tone which makes any cook long to crack skulls with a frying pan. I grew to dread these excursions of Lucien's into haute cuisine. They so often ended with a discouraged look in the old man's eyes.

One evening when Lucien had slaved over crepes suzette for that bunch of ravenous loggers, a joker remarked in a loud voice, "Old Fox better see that Cookie gets himself some sleep. He thinks it's breakfast." There were even some ill-natured grumblings from the older hands.

Lucien walked out of the kitchen carrying Boygen, his kitten and did not emerge the next day until noon. The kitchen crew retaliated against the whole camp. We attacked the soft underbelly by serving the most meager breakfast we could and hiding the pies and cakes from the lunch tables.

By that time I had come to feel a great protectiveness toward Lucien. His past so clearly had held discouragement enough to last any man a lifetime.

In spite of his bad leg, he was forever in the kitchen, still working when we left at night, with Boygen curled up on the padded powder box Lucien had fixed for him. Generally cats are unpopular in a logging camp, and absolutely taboo in a cookhouse. It was only the desperate need for a cook and the firm set of Lucien's jaw which had made Old Fox swallow his protest when he first laid eyes on Boygen. As it was, our boss kept a suspicious eye on the kitten expecting to catch him on a table. He never did. Boygen could be trusted even when there was meat on the chopping block. After all, he lived a Lucullan existence, all the kidney and beef liver he could eat and, if we were out of that, the morsels of filet mignon. He was growing up to be a great beauty, too, with yellow, silky fur and a big white ruff framing his pixie face.

"Run along now, all of you," Lucien would say after supper. "Get yourselves some rest. The baby Boygen will keep me company. Isn't that so, little one?"

The cat would stare steadily up at Lucien out of his topaz eyes until I half suspected he understood.

In the morning there would be rows of delicious pastries lined up on the pieboard when we came in.

Sometimes I would try to run a little interference when Lucien produced the unexpected for supper—on the night, for example, when he served celery Victor. I knew the loggers would not like celery Victor, particularly after Lucien had me hurry around, placing a strip of anchovy filet on each salad plate. When the men were seated, I lurked as near the dining-room door as possible and the moment a man reared back and said, "What the HELL!" I hurried right in.

"That's an anchovy," I said. "It's *supposed* to be there." I knew perfectly well he thought it was some horrid thing dropped on his salad by mistake.

"A which?"

"An anchovy. Taste it," I urged.

He picked it up gingerly and took a bite while the other men at the table stopped eating and watched him intently.

"It's fish," he said and as the full flavor hit him he made a gagging face and grabbed for his coffee cup to drown the taste. Every man then carefully picked off the anchovy and put it to one side of his plate. All except the Bull Buck. The Bull Buck, of all unlikely people, turned out to be something of a gourmet. He was a powerful man, big enough to hunt bear with a switch, whose face looked sort of unfinished, as if someone had made a hasty sketch and then not bothered to go on with it. But he had traveled widely during World War II and perhaps in strange foreign ports had learned to enjoy unusual flavors. He used to stop around at the cookhouse of an evening and talk food with Lucien.

I loved to hear Lucien talking food, even though most of the information was quite useless to me. I do not think I will ever be called upon to mask a salmon and I am quite sure I will never use the knowledge that a female pompano is superior to the male, since we do not have pompano on the Pacific Coast. But it was a delight to hear him speak of the gay little condiments which contrast so beautifully with the deep, full-bodied flavors, of the little surprise which every meal should contain and of the exquisite harmony inherent in a good sauce. You would have thought he was talking about a concerto.

Lucien could be a spellbinder when he wanted to be. They'd sit there together at the little kitchen table, the huge Bull Buck dreamily stirring his spoon around in his coffee, and Lucien in his apron, holding his kitten. They would speak of curries and of lobsters and of wine. Their talk covered the world and listening, I could almost see fishermen hauling in their nets full of flopping, shining fish; great round cheeses; fruit ripening under a tropic sun or smell the deep, rich perfume of the grape. Through it all ran Boygen's constant throaty purr.

Nor did Lucien's innovations always fall flat with the loggers, either. On one occasion, when we were having steaks and the ovens were free, Lucien decided to make twelve chocolate soufflés for supper, one for each table. I was not worried about the reception of the soufflés. Although most of the loggers probably never had eaten one, still chocolate is a universal flavor. They had been sucking on candy bars since babyhood.

Lucien insisted on presenting the soufflés with ceremony. First he had Midge and Bonny place the sauce on each table. Then he lined us up, with me in front because I was the smallest, followed by Bonny and Midge and John Paul bringing up the rear. At a signal from Lucien, we all paraded into the dining room, each of us carrying a great soufflé, majestically risen. It made quite a sensation. When all the tables were served, we hung about near the door anxiously waiting while Lucien stood back by the stove, as tense as if he had just served Edward VII.

The reaction came instantly. "Oh boy, oh boy, oh boy," I heard one logger exclaim at the first mouthful. That was followed by a perfect explosion of "Wow's!" Bless their hearts, at least a dozen stuck their heads into the kitchen afterwards to say, "That sure was a swell pudding, Cookie."

Lucien received this acclaim with courtly dignity, but his old eyes lit up. He had the most wonderful brown eyes, soft as a caress when he looked at Boygen, but if I did something stupid a glance out of them could make me quail, and when he was really angry I imagined I could hear them crackle.

One Sunday morning as I came into the cookhouse, there was such an earth-shaking explosion off in the distance that my very teeth seemed to rattle around in my head. Boygen, who had been sitting sleepily on the back steps, bounded into the brush and raced up a young fir tree and John Paul sprinted out to the porch. "What in thunder? An earthquake?"

Midge had the answer. She always knew what was going on in camp. She said they were probably blasting Hell's Corridor. They were going to use a ton of dynamite in one blast, she said, and they wanted to get it done on Sunday so they would not tie up the road Monday morning.

I already knew an overhanging rock in Hell's Corridor was dangerous. Wild Bill had said: "The log trucks got to get down on their knees and sneak through when the rocks ain't looking."

After the men came in for breakfast, I could hear Old Fox chewing out Hans, the road boss. The road, I gathered, was now completely submerged under a mountain of displaced rock.

Hans just kept on grinning, every gold tooth in his big mouth showing.

"Vell, ven I shoot dem, dey stay shot," he said.

"Don't act so goddamn happy about it. Want to stop the work now of all times?"

Hans shrugged. "Dat new powder monkey ain't vert a damn. Der vas youst a "faul-it" and ven ve blasted der bloomin mountain all piled up."

"You better unpile it, and damn fast. Get every man in camp on it right away. In the morning when the crew is back, get every goddamn Cat on it, plus the shovel and all the trucks you need. What in hell ever made you think you're a road builder anyway?"

"Dat rock vas youst as pig as a house—"

"Okay, okay, but the road has *got* to be opened by to-morrow night, understand?"

"Maybe." Hans's face was stubborn. "I'm de road boss and dot is dot!"

Old Fox brought his cup of coffee into the kitchen, as if he knew he would fire Hans if he stayed another minute.

The crew, coming from town Sunday night, were forced to leave the crummies on the other side of the slide and hike the five miles to camp. I doubt if such a sobered crew had ever arrived in camp after a weekend. Swivelneck, driving out with the supplies, had to return to town, leaving Lucien out of fresh meat and growing madder every minute. Monday night the Corridor was still closed.

During the supper rush Lucien limped out into the dining room. There was a sudden hush, forks stopped halfway to loggers' mouths. For the cook to come into the dining rooms during a meal was an unheard-of thing.

In the silence, Lucien faced Hans. "Hans, that road—when will she be open?"

"Vell," Hans said, "I'll tell you. I youst don't know."

"That road, she had better be open very, very quick." Lucien's voice was actually quivering with rage. "Tomorrow night, you understand, a little pig of yours will be on every table. With an apple in its mouth." He turned around and limped out.

Hans's grin seemed to grow fixed on his face and slowly curdled into a grimace of pain. The Corridor was cleared by noon the next day. Hans went even further. He hurriedly had a big, comfortable pen made for the hogs, probably to keep them from getting underfoot and tempting Lucien.

After Lucien had been in camp for two weeks, I weighed myself and found I had gained back five pounds. All that weight did not come from gourmandizing on his food, either. Feeling light hearted had a great deal to do with it. I felt so light hearted I was downright irresponsible. I even let Midge and Bonny persuade me, one afternoon, to hike up the river for a mile or so where Midge's Reese Downey was going to rig a tree.

Women are not welcome around the works. We all had orders to keep away from them on weekdays. But I decided this day was different. In the first place, Old Fox and Camp Push had both gone to the Bay on business. Besides, a new landing was being readied, so things were not really in full swing. Reese-the-Rig had issued a special invitation and, as Midge's fiancé, this seemed to make it more acceptable. Anyway, that's what I told myself when we started off.

A landing is a location which has been leveled by a bulldozer and is used for loading logs onto trucks by means of a rigged sparpole and a loading bitch. Reese was going to top a tree for the sparpole, the only reason why a tree is ever topped, in spite of the logging movies where men seem to go around topping them right and left.

We tried to sneak up on the landing to watch the loggers unobserved. Unfortunately, Bonny tripped over a root and rolled almost in front of Indian Johnny's bulldozer.

Boo-boo number one, I thought as Johnny shut off the Cat and yelled out, "Hey, you scairt the daylights out of me." He looked around uneasily. "You gals better get up here. I got to do some work on the durn blade anyway."

We all clambered up hilariously. The clearing was about a hundred and fifty feet in diameter and smelled of freshly scraped earth, the same nice smell I remembered from my childhood when I used to trot along behind Dad's plow sniffing the fragrant moist soil. A tree some four feet in diameter had been left in the center of the clearing. Reese already had trimmed off the lower branches and begun to work his way up the tree, wearing climbing spurs and a safety belt around both himself and the tree. The safety belt, Midge explained, had a steel core because too many high climbers in the past had cut off their own belts with their axes. Reese's ax hung from a four-foot rope on one side of his belt, a one-man crosscut saw on the other. When he had dug his spurs into the tree, he would lean back against the belt and, with his ax, chop off all the limbs he could reach above him. Then he would put his ax back in its holder to free both hands, grasp the safety rope at arm's length and with a flipping motion work it further up the tree. Chop, chop—down went the limbs. Toss, step, toss, step—up went the rope and Reese. The tree was limby and the pile around its base grew higher and higher, as if it were keeping pace with the climber.

Reese saw us sitting on the Cat and waved. His tin hat had fallen off and I could see his red hair standing up straight as he swayed so high above us. Finally he had worked his way a hundred feet above the ground. The limbs he had chopped off looked like a fur collar around the tree, or like a tall haystack with a telephone pole sticking out of the middle. When he moved around the tree he appeared to be cutting directly into it. "He's undercutting now," Midge said, as proudly as if she were doing it herself.

As he pulled up the short saw and started the tricky job of sawing off the treetop, all the men stopped work to stand watching. It seemed an endless wait before the feathered top tipped slowly, almost as if it were hanging its head in shame, then broke loose and tumbled downward, leaving a jagged splinter at the top.

I could see the whole tree vibrate for an instant, while Reese rested his weight against the safety belt, before he took his ax and made short work of the splinter. The sparpole seemed perfect to me. Apparently it did not quite suit Reese. Or possibly the sight of Midge below him, her hands clasped over her head in the winner's gesture, egged him on to show off a bit. Anyway, he started to go a little higher, turning to look down at us as he grabbed the safety rope in both hands. Toss, step, toss, step—it seemed completely effortless from where we sat watching. And then suddenly, the rope took wings. It flew over the topped tree and hung for an instant like a gruesome cobweb above Reese's head. I could see Reese's arms clutching at the limbless tree before he turned, end over end, and dropped like a winged duck.

Midge gave one moan, and then she was off the Cat in a single leap and racing toward the sparpole. We were all right behind her. Reese-the-Rig had disappeared completely in the loose pile of limbs, but as we reached the tree, his red head thrust its way up through the boughs.

"That was a corny thing to do," he said, his grin lopsided, as he clawed his way to the top.

"Oh darling, lie still," Midge cried.

"I'm all right, honey. Bent a little, but not busted. Sure a lucky thing the old gal was a real limby so-and-so." He was struggling to get up.

"No you don't," the hook tender ordered. "Hey," he bellowed. "Bring the stretcher from the half-track. We're going to pack this kid out of here to the crummy."

Nobody said, at least in our hearing, "Damn those fool women for hanging around and putting a jinx on the works."

But I damned myself, thoroughly and completely, even though Reese was almost right about his injuries. The only things "busted" were a couple of ribs and in no time at all it seemed to me, he was back climbing, as gay as ever.

But in the meantime, Midge walked around like a zombie. "She loves very much," Lucien said with approval. He picked up Boygen and cradled the kitten in his arms and I thought: Now we're three of a kind, Lucien with his kitten, John Paul with his ghostly Agnes and I with two old letters and a photograph. Yet there were almost a hundred living, breathing men I could have had my pick of, with a little trouble and attention to details. Well, put the figure at fifty, just to be on the safe side. It was still a staggering number. All a woman had to do was look steadily, a little longer than necessary, into a pair of lonely logging eyes to see the hope starting in them.

That night I got out Gina's music box and sat on the porch of the Old Homestead, the way Gina used to do. When I wound the box, the tinkling little tune spilled out into the night, so gay, so wonderfully gay, and yet with the undertone of sadness all music boxes seem to have. I could see crazy young Gina, running out into the darkness, braving the bear and cougar, and I could see Reese-the-Rig's face, white below the brush of red hair as it poked up through the pile of limbs, and hear him say, "I'm all right, honey," even while looking up at Midge for reassurance.

Love, love, love, love, that's all the fool music box would play. I was winding it for the third time when Edison Smith came by. All I was thinking about at the moment was love and how I didn't have any myself, so naturally I studied him to try to imagine what loving Edison would be like. Well, why not? I asked myself. A big, kindly man like that.

Edison had nice plans for my weekend off. The next afternoon, Friday, he was going to drive me into town; on Saturday night he would come around and take me to the dance at the Elks Club. And on Sunday, he said, rather hesitantly, if I liked the idea, he would drive me over to look at his tree farm.

As soon as he had left I walked into the Old Homestead, jerked my valise out from under my cot and pulled out the photograph and the two letters. I did not read the letters or look at the picture. I tore them into small pieces, went out the back door, dug a hole in the earth and buried them. On top of the mound I wrote with a stick, faintly so nobody else could read it: "Here lies Doug Weatherby. Requiescat in Pace."

And that is that, I told myself. Now it is all over. I listened to my heart, the way Gina used to do, and it seemed to respond reassuringly. Almost.

Snoozy the bull cook was also going to town that Friday for the first time in nearly six months. Payday marked the halfway point in his goal of seven thousand and the whole camp had been hearing about it for a week. He was going to ride down with the men in one of the crummies. I was in the cookhouse, ready to start off with Edison, when old Snoozy rushed in, his eyes bright with anger and the shine on his shoes even brighter. He was almost crying. "They've gone and left me. I missed the last damn crummy."

"But you started to get ready an hour ago," Edison said.

"Some goddamn ape nailed my shoes to the floor." His poor, raddled old face looked as if it were going to dissolve any minute.

"It's all right, Snoozy," Edison said. "You can ride in with us." He hesitated a second. "If you're sure you want to go," he added.

"Damn right I want to go," Snoozy snapped. "For God's sake, don't you think I can be trusted in the big city? Afraid I'll strain my neck looking at that one tall building, for God's sake, or go blind when I see all those bright lights?"

"Swell," I said. "You go with us. We can all strain our necks at the same time."

Snoozy began to look a little less belligerent. He gave a hitch to his natty town pants. "Say," he said suddenly, as if a proud idea had just struck him, "why don't you and Ed have dinner with me? I'll have fifty, sixty dollars left after I make my deposit. We can get a real meal at the Chandler."

Nobody could see that toothless smile and disappoint the old man. "Why," I stammered, "it sounds like fun."

"Okay by me," Edison said. "If you're sure you want to go." He still sounded worried.

"Don't be such an old woman," Snoozy said. "Let's go." He held the door open for me with an air of extreme elegance, and all the way to town kept up an incessant chatter from the back seat about his plans for the weekend. They seemed to include every possible form of entertainment except stops at a tavern.

Edison pulled up in front of the bank. The parking meter said "expired" and there was not a nickel, dime or penny among us. Just large greenbacks.

"I'll get some change," I said. "I'm mailing my check to San Francisco this month."

It was almost closing time and a line had formed at every window. Fully ten minutes passed before I got back with change and found a parking ticket on the car. I had it stowed away in my purse by the time the others came out of the bank and climbed in. Snoozy passed his bank book around, with the balance now over $3500. "Personalized checks," he said grandly.

"Drive up past City Hall, will you, Edison?" I asked as noncommittally as I could.

"Heck, you can't get a marriage license there!" Snoozy yelled out from the back seat.

Edison turned around and looked at me. "I'll bet we got a parking ticket. Hand it over."

"This," I said, "is my own private parking ticket. You can't have it."

"Don't be silly, Lee," Edison told me. "Give it here."

When I pulled the ticket out of my purse there was a wild explosion from the back seat. "Those dirty, rotten cops," Snoozy roared out. "The goddamn sons of bitches. They do it every time. They're on my trail as soon as I hit town—"

"The ticket's not for you, Snoozy," I said.

"Don't give me that phony baloney. It's a goddamn frameup. Here, give me that. I have a few pennies left. Those bastards won't be satisfied until they get my last crying dime." He snatched the ticket out of my hand as we pulled up in front of City Hall and, leaping out of the car, took the stone steps two at a time.

Edison looked after his outraged figure disappearing through the doors. "Working himself up to a thirst," he said somberly.

"Oh no!" I cried.

"It happens every time," Edison went on. "This is the longest he's been sober for ten years."

"But can't we do *something?*" I insisted.

Edison shook his head. "Nothing short of hog-tying him."

"He wants that trip home so much, too." I felt like crying.

"I don't think he really wants to go home," Edison said unexpectedly. "That's just something to dream about. He probably knows he wouldn't have a thing in common with his family any more. It would be a misery all around. He's happy enough making the loggers' beds and sweeping their floors and hanging up their wet clothes to dry, clucking around like a mother hen trying to take care of a nest of ducklings. He knew all the time he'd have to go on a bender before his dream got too real. The parking ticket was the first excuse that came along."

"I wish we could get hold of his checkbook," I said unhappily.

"That wouldn't do any good, either. He's known all over town. The cafes and the taverns and even the pigs seem to know when to stop writing checks for him to sign."

Snoozy came out madder than a wet hen. "By God, I told those cops a thing or two," he raged, climbing into the car. "I told them this was once when I wouldn't wind up in their filthy jail with money in my pockets for them to pick. Just a goddamn bunch of pickpockets—I told them so, too. Say, Ed, let me out here on Broadway. I promised I'd see Indian Johnny at Jug's. I owe him some money."

As he started down the sidewalk I made one last effort. "What about our date at the Chandler?" I called after him.

He walked back to the car and held a twenty-dollar bill out to Edison. I had never seen a sadder pair of eyes in my life. "You take her, Edison. I may get tied up."

To my surprise, Edison took the money. When Snoozy had vanished through the swinging doors at Jug's Tavern, he put the twenty in a separate compartment of his billfold. "This will keep him in snoose and smokes until next payday," he said. "Swivelneck always rags the hell out of him when he's broke."

That was the last we saw of Snoozy for two days. We did have dinner at the Chandler that Friday in order to tell him about it later. But Saturday was the big night. I wore the extravagant I. Magnin dinner dress I had brought up from San Francisco and, as the ultimate touch of elegance, I stuck on a whole set of artificial fingernails, so long they would have made an ancient Chinese gentleman look like a coolie. Nobody could possibly have guessed my hands had ever been near bread dough, pie dough or, for that matter, a cook stove, either. I painted my bogus nails gold, to go with my hair and to tone pleasantly with the shades of jade and blue of my dress.

To my delight Edison looked absolutely overwhelmed at the sight of me, that is until he saw my fancy fingers and then I thought he was going to choke with laughter.

"Are they that funny?" I felt a little squelched. I had no intention of starting all the Elks howling with laughter when we entered the hall. "I can take them off," I said uncertainly.

"No, no, they're beautiful," he managed to gasp.

I started to put my room key in my purse and stopped, a little bewildered. How on earth do you open a purse when your fingernails are an inch long? With the teeth, perhaps, I thought. But that didn't seem quite right, either. I would look pretty silly standing there in the hotel lobby furiously biting at an evening purse.

I handed purse and key to Edison. "I'm afraid you'll have to do it," I said in a meek voice.

By the end of the evening I suspected Gina was right and that Edison really was in love with me. The next day I knew it. The day was perfect for our excursion to his tree farm. There had been a cold snap, just enough to splash the countryside with the red and orange of vine maple, and then a warm chinook had come, bringing Indian summer with it.

We crossed the river by ferry, the same old scowlike ferry I remembered from my childhood, with the same ruddy-faced genial Captain Andy starting up the motor as soon as we reached the ferry slip. Edison was rather tense, it seemed to me, as we drove along the lower river, but by that time I was lost in memories. Before the roads were built, we always traveled to school on the milk boats and I knew every lovely bend we passed.

At Allegany we turned onto the narrow Millicoma road, edging its way high above the little river which threaded between the green cliffs below. Once we drove under the branches of a large-leafed maple and its leafy shadow capered on the road. On each side were well-spaced firs and clumps of Christmas ferns, vivid green against the darker moss.

Some three miles above Allegany, Edison stopped the jeep by a meadow and I bounced out. Across the road from the meadow a level strip, rising gradually into hills, was covered by young firs, recently thinned and trimmed and wonderfully well tended. But it was the meadow itself which caught me speechless by its beauty, two acres of it, sloping to the river. Directly across, a forty-foot waterfall plunged down a cliff, frothing the pool it formed. All around it rising up the low hill, vine maple and dogwood blazed orange and crimson against the glossy myrtles and the green of firs.

Toward the north end of the field, the meadow slanted toward a sassy little creek. The elders lining its banks were already shedding their leaves and their gray and white bark made a frame for the luminous water. And there stood the fir tree. It is perfectly possible to fall in love with a tree at first sight. I did. This one was old, its north limbs dipping to follow the contour of the land. On one limb hung an abandoned oriole's nest, lopsided with its hood of sticks and moss.

I glanced at Edison. He smiled at me for a minute and then he walked over, just south of the beautiful fir and directly across from the waterfall. "How do you like this for a homesite?" he asked.

Like it! I thought. I was way ahead of him. The house had already risen right up there in my mind, even the sunken garden, the little wild violets and the trillium, shaded by the bending branches of the fir. In the spring, the white dogwood blossoms would look like stars against the dark trees and the orioles would come back to their nest. All year long the air would be forest scented and the river would croon past our door.

But the darndest thing was, I couldn't say it. I knew I was not mistaken in his meaning or the expression in his eyes. But all I could do was stand there feeling blank. And when the silence had stretched out until I could not stand it anymore, I pointed stupidly to a shack which I imagined he had used on his working vacations. "What's the matter with that little gray home in the West?" I babbled.

The glow went out of Edison's face. "Well," he said, smiling a little wryly, "what about lunch?"

So we picnicked in front of the falls on the lunch Edison had had made up in town. A good lunch, too—cold roast pork sandwiches with dill pickles and stuffed green olives, little jars of apple sauce and a thermos jug of coffee. He had even latched onto a wild blackberry pie. Edison talked gaily enough about the loggers he had seen in town, about Snoozy and Old Fox and Swivelneck, and I kept still about the bottle of champagne I had seen hidden in the back of the jeep in a bucket of ice. Edison did not produce the champagne. The champagne must have been for a celebration and today there was not to be a celebration, after all.

When we drove back through Coos Bay he stopped in front of City Hall and said, "Well, we might as well pick up Snoozy. I'll see if he's in jail. They'll release him to me all right."

A few minutes later he helped a limp, dirty, sick Snoozy down the steps and practically lifted him into the back seat. Snoozy did not say a word all the way back to camp, except for an occasional groan or curse. It was a relief when he started to snore steadily.

On Monday morning he came to table, pallid and dolorous, and drank copiously of the tomato juice and black coffee. By Wednesday he was his usual blithe self and within a month he showed me figures in a little black book where he had worked out just how long it would take him to save $7000 so he could go down to Oakland to see his family and make a big splash.

chapter ten

OUR Indian summer stayed with us, lovely and warm, with no sudden windstorms to add extra danger to the logging. The Ticoma, I heard, was known all over the district as a damn good camp, and no wonder, with the sort of food we served the loggers.

Lucien continued to cook with zest and passion—magnificent ham omelets, for example, light and airy as a dream. The loggers even grew to relish broccoli when served with Lucien's superb hollandaise sauce. On the Bull Buck's birthday I had a moment's qualm, wondering if the poor old man had gone over the edge. When I came into the cookhouse I discovered he had baked and frosted twelve great towering cakes, each one resembling, of all things, a castle in Spain. I never did understand the significance of this.

Lucien again insisted on a processional and I must say it was a brave sight, the Bull Buck's cake all ablaze with forty-three candles stuck around the battlements and a hundred loggers roaring out at the top of their tremendous lungs: "Happy Birthday, dear Bull Buck."

Naturally we had our little ups and downs, too. The camp was under continual pressure to get the orders out; there were some fights and the usual amount of beefing, but the work rolled ahead as smoothly as work can ever roll when it involves a hundred men. Or so it seemed to me.

One evening our coffee hounds were engaged in the usual horseplay in the cookhouse. A big, particularly tough bucker had stuck two cantaloupes inside his T-shirt at strategic places and was clowning around with a floor mop held up behind him. Its top dangled over his head like messy curls and he was singing in a booming basso profundo, "For I am the Queen of the May, tra-la," skipping about the room, his face twisted into a girlish simper. The great clump of his feet and that horrendous voice sounded as if a herd of bull moose had been let loose among us.

In other words, everything was perfectly normal that night at the Ticoma logging camp, until Camp Push came in. Camp Push did not look normal at all. His usually shy eyes were blazing. "Can any of you guys give me some idea what's going on around this camp?" he demanded.

We stopped whatever we were doing and stared at him blankly.

"Some son of a bitch has opened up the fuel sleds. Punched holes in half a dozen diesel tanks." He glanced around at our startled faces. "We used up all our diesel today. That means nothing can move tomorrow until the truck gets here in the morning."

He took a deep breath as if he were trying to steady himself. "Just what the *hell* goes on?"

The big bucker still held the mop up behind him, as if he had forgotten it, but the melons had worked their way down inside his T-shirt until they were at his stomach line. "Somebody punched them holes on purpose?"

"It sure as hell wasn't any accident," Push exploded. His shoulders were hunched up and his hands thrust into his pockets in fists. "As you know, last week number three donkey froze up. You found it was sugar in the oil, didn't you, Jake?"

"Some polecat sure sweetened her," Moonshine Jake said, nodding his bald head. "That dad-burned motor ran till Bob Botts shut her off for a coffee break. When he tried to start it again it was stuck solid. That blamed sugar had burnt and you never saw such a mess. The mechanics and I had to take it all apart and scrape and polish—"

"Yeah," interrupted an aggrieved choker setter, "we lost two whole days' work."

I had heard about the trouble with number three. The subject had been dismissed with a string of strong words and the remark that somebody must have it in for one of the donkey crew. But punching holes in half a dozen tanks certainly did not sound like a private feud.

"This stuff isn't the work of any jackassical joker trying to be funny," Camp Push said. "Either we've got a nut in camp or somebody's deliberately trying to louse up the works. You guys got any suspicions?"

Nobody had.

"Well," Push said, "if we don't get to the bottom of it we'll be out of business." He went on to explain that we were behind in our orders as it was and unless everybody was alert to prevent more mischief, we were headed for real disaster. It was the longest speech I had ever heard Push make. He said if we didn't get out every log possible, we would be short when it came time to splash and then we were all sunk.

"Splashing" was the big log drive when the river dam was opened and the logs started on their trip downriver to the Bay.

"We'll all keep our eyes open, Push," Edison said.

"It's not only Coos Pacific that will get it in the neck," Push said. "If we can't fill our order, the camp will shut down tight and every damn logger will be out of a job." The floor shook as he stalked out of the cookhouse.

"I sure feel sorry for the jerk when Push catches him," Edison said. "When Push gets riled, he's *mad.*"

"But why the heck?" the bucker said, in outrage. "Who'd want to pull stunts like that?"

"While we're playing guessing games," Indian Johnny put in, "how come Swivelneck claims to have bought a spool of one and a quarter inch cable and no one will admit hauling it out and no one's been able to find it?"

No one had an answer to that, either.

"The hell of it," Wild Bill said, "is that both those stunts were pulled at night. Who the devil is going to baby-sit the whole works at night?"

"I'll guard number three," Bob Botts said unexpectedly. "I can sleep up there. I've got a sleeping bag."

The loggers studied him without enthusiasm for a minute, before somebody said rather grudgingly, "Maybe that's a pretty good idea." Bob Botts got a self-righteous look on his face. The loggers had been giving him the silent treatment ever since the fight when he had banged Reese-the-Rig over the head with a club.

"Well," Indian Johnny said, "I guess I can stick pretty close to my Cat."

"Nerts to that," Moonshine Jake cried out, the old Wobbly in him aroused instantly. "If the company wants guards, they can durn well hire 'em."

Most of the crew agreed with Moonshine Jake. Their day was long enough, the work often punishing and they needed rest to be alert on their jobs. Just the same, I could understand how Bob Botts and Indian Johnny felt.

I went to bed worrying about my own course of action. I could not decide if I should report something I had seen to Old Fox and Camp Push. The memory was very vague and I could not put a name to the man, but stirring around in the back of my mind was the picture of loggers filling their lunch buckets and of somebody pouring a ridiculous amount of sugar into his thermos bottle. Possibly there hadn't been any coffee in the bottle at all. Just sugar to gum up a machine.

I tried to make the picture more vivid in my mind. Nothing emerged but the memory of jostling men and that steady stream of sugar pouring into a thermos bottle. We had so many new men, I thought in discouragement, and some of them were pretty strange characters. Like the Preacher and the Bear.

I had seen the two arrive several weeks before when I was in the commissary buying hand soap. They had stopped to ask Swivelneck where they were supposed to bunk. They were a striking pair. One was tall, thin as a willow wand and of solemn mien, dressed in conservative tweeds and a white shirt, the like of which was seldom seen around the Ticoma. The other, who hung along behind the first, was a huge, bear-shaped man with arms bulging like overstuffed pillows and dressed in Paul Bunyan style, with a red-checked shirt and stagged levis. His boots added a bizarre note, being only half laced. But it was his face which gave me the willies. The whole face seemed to sag like a piece of raw beef held up by one end. His nose was flattened and shoved off at an angle; there were lumps of scar tissue over his ragged eyebrows, and his ears, four times as thick as normal, were almost completely closed.

I took one look and got out of the commissary fast because he began right away to grin at me, nudging the lean man and muttering, "Pipe the skirt. She wiggles real cute.

Yeah, she sure wiggles real cute." His voice sounded thick as if it were coming through layers of cotton.

I was *not* wiggling which made the remark all the more preposterous.

Since loggers have an absolute mania for colorful nicknames, the pair had not been in camp twenty-four hours before they were known as the Preacher and the Bear. The two were never apart, the Bear always watching, as if he hoped someone would stir up a storm and he would have a chance to defend his partner. Even the loggers, who revere strength and are the most tolerant group on earth, felt he was an oddball. None of them, not even Indian Johnny with his tremendous strength, made an excuse to test his hitting ability.

"He's punchy as hell," Indian Johnny said at our coffee session. "I'm not going out of my way to rile that creep, that's for sure."

"Well," Wild Bill said, "he sure don't track too good in his thinking, but I never see him stumbling around or stuff like that."

Strange stories came in from the woods. The men said whenever he was startled he would swing a savage punch or two. Any sudden noise, a whistle, a shout or a board dropped behind him, would set him off. "Reflexes all shot to hell," they said.

Whenever I passed him I would hear him talking about what a fighter he had been: "I'm fightin' de Sailor, see? One more fight and I take on de champ. I'm beatin' hell outta de Sailor when bang! an' I get one. I look around, but I don't see nobody."

Several times we noticed the Bear peering in at the cookhouse windows as we were getting supper. To my annoyance he seemed to be peering particularly at me. Seeing his head ducking back and forth out there, I kept wondering if he had come because I "wiggled cute." I found myself walking around the kitchen stiff as a ramrod, moving only from the knees down. I would glance quickly over my shoulder, see that poor slob of a face with a grin on it at the window and feel a cold chill run along my spine.

Naturally when I asked myself who had been trying to sabotage the works, I thought first of the Preacher and the Bear. And yet I could not fit either of them into my memory of the sugared thermos bottle. The hands stopped me. Both the Preacher and the Bear had noticeable hands, the Preacher's soft looking and unusually well kept for a logger, the Bear's badly knobbed, as if they had been broken several times from hitting too hard. If either had been holding the thermos bottle or the sugar bowl, I felt sure the sight of the hands would have stayed with me. Instead, my recollection was of something quite ordinary, just anybody's hands. I decided to let the picture lie undisturbed at the bottom of my mind. Possibly my subconscious would work on it. Other people seemed able to solve their problems by means of the subconscious mind. My own subconscious never did any useful work, as far as I could see, but I was willing to give it a try.

Two days after Camp Push paid his visit to the cookhouse, the crew found three cables cut on the Rock Creek sparpole. That crew lost half a day's work.

With a mystery in camp, Swivelneck was right in his element, gumshoeing all over the place. He prowled the works during the day and sometimes, it was rumored, at night. He took to heckling Lucien about food which he claimed had been bought and had never showed up, a case of olives, a side of beef and so on. He even came pussyfooting over to the cookhouse in the evening to listen in on the conversations. As soon as he appeared, the talk would die down, someone would start a song or the loggers would put their coffee cups in the sink and drift out.

Before long the camp buzzed about a feud between Swivelneck and the Preacher. One logger claimed Swivelneck had been on the point of taking a poke at the Preacher.

"With the Bear standing guard!" Bob Botts snorted. "Old Swivel may be nosy, but he's not that crazy."

"Who's scaling for them, anyway?" Snoozy asked of no one in particular.

"What the hell's the difference?" Wild Bill sounded disgusted. "Swivelneck is always suspicious of every scaler. I say when you're busheling you *got* to trust the scaler."

I knew the Preacher and the Bear were working as a team, falling and bucking. "Busheling" meant they felled the trees, sawed them into log lengths, and were paid by the number of board feet the scaler measured with his "swindle" stick. The Preacher and the Bear were doing very well indeed.

One afternoon I stopped at the commissary and found a pair of fallers and buckers there. One of them had Swivelneck backed up against the counter. His two big hands were around Swivelneck's throat and he was saying, "You want to show me that log scale sheet or you want me to choke hell out of you?"

If I had thought the bucker was going to choke Swivelneck to death I would have shrieked my head off. The gesture seemed to me more in the way of an admonition, so I simply watched with interest.

Swivelneck groped around behind him and pulled out a paper. The two men immediately let go of him and bent over the worksheet.

"Look!" one of them yelled. "I worked Saturday to get

time and a half and it says here all I made was forty dollars! Hell, I could beat that using a hand briar."

"Looka here at the Bear's scale! He made ninety-six dollars that same day."

The two angry red faces turned toward each other in mutual outrage for an instant. Then both men went pushing through the door swearing they were going to find the scaler and beat hell out of him.

Swivelneck did not seem in the least disturbed. He stood, gently massaging his throat and looking amused. "They won't find the scaler," he said. "He left for the Midwest yesterday. His old man died."

I could not imagine why this should be the cause of so much satisfaction to Swivelneck unless he did not want the fallers to beat the truth out of a dishonest scaler. Maybe he wanted to discover the culprit on his own and be a hero in the eyes of the company. Then I remembered the utility cow Swivelneck had listed as prime beef and wondered uneasily if he were up to his ears in some dirty work himself, using his gumshoeing and his reputation as a company man as a blind.

Within a week two more pieces of skulduggery occurred. Another motor was sugared and the airline on a logging trailer was hooked on backward. As the men explained to me, air brakes without air are like hydraulic brakes without brake fluid. The unsuspecting truck driver coming down a steep hill escaped by bailing out, but the truck and its valuable load of peelers were in the bottom of a deep canyon.

Up to this point the damage had caused expensive delay. But this time a new element was present. The life of the driver had been endangered and in the eyes of the camp that was quite another kettle of fish. I could feel the uneasiness all around me. The only thing anybody talked about was "Where will the sons of bitches strike next?" I'd see the truckers giving their trucks a thorough going-over before starting out, particularly the air-brake hoses. Donkey punchers fingered their motor oil feeling for a trace of sugar before starting the motors; catskinners went over the Cats inch by inch, and every foreman and side boss kept a weather eye peeled. Old Fox was always around camp in those days.

I kept remembering Camp Push's remark. He had said there might be a nut in camp. Not a pleasant thought and I began to worry again about the bolt on my door. A most ineffectual bolt. The wood had rotted around the screws until any good hefty shove would have knocked them right out. I had always felt perfectly secure with the year-round or home crew, but three weeks before a new worker had been assigned to a bunkhouse near the Old Homestead and having a stranger bunking so close gave me the jitters.

"Just take a case knife," John Paul had told me. "Turn the handle toward the center of your door, shove the point of the knife under the casing and you got a good bolt. I kept out a guy that way once when he ran amok in Singapore."

I tried the trick on the kitchen door and it worked perfectly. That night, feeling like a fool, I picked out a thin case knife, hid it under my apron (I certainly did not want to advertise my maidenly terrors) and slipped it out of the cookhouse. I had almost reached my cabin when I stopped in astonishment. The new man, with his lantern on the ground beside him, was busily putting a lock on *his* door.

This struck me as uproariously funny. I tossed my knife onto a shelf in the Old Homestead and forgot it. But with all the hocus-pocus going on in camp and the general sense of something very wrong, I got out the knife later and every night shoved it under the door casing.

One night I woke up fancying I had felt a mild earthquake. For a moment I lay still, puzzled, and then suddenly sat up in bed. Heavy feet had crossed my rickety porch and stopped in front of my door. After that there was silence until, straining my ears, I heard a faint creak, as if someone had shifted his weight a little. I grabbed my nail scissors from the powder-box nightstand, slipped out of bed and tiptoed to the window. When I pulled the curtain aside the barest crack I could make out a big lump of a shadow almost against the door. It looked like a bear. He turned his great head and it *was* the Bear.

If he lifts his hand to the door knob, I'll scream bloody murder and leap out the back window, I told myself. But I did not know if I could move. I did not know if I could even scream. My throat seemed to have closed up tight. And the thoughts moved very slowly through my head. My nail scissors won't be worth a thing, I thought. The case knife barring the door isn't worth a thing, either. One heave of those shoulders would bring the door itself right down.

For a few harrowing moments he stood indecisively there and then he turned and, shadow boxing in the moonlight, walked away. I flew around the cabin, propping a chair under the front door knob, trying the back door to make sure the bolt there held and scrambled into bed, shaking all over with terror now that I was perfectly safe. And yet by the next morning I had decided not to tell anybody about the night's alarm. I couldn't quite put my finger on the reason. I just knew I didn't want to mention it. Instead, I asked Snoozy please to put a new and better lock on my door.

That Sunday Lucien had one of his migraine headaches.

Midge and Bonny had gone to Sumner for the afternoon and it was John Paul's regular time off. Only a handful of men had stayed in camp, so I decided to bake French apple pies for supper.

As I started to form the graham-cracker crusts, a stranger walked into the cookhouse. "Would I be upsetting your schedule if I begged a bite to eat?" he asked pleasantly, so pleasantly that I felt anxious to be agreeable too. He was an unusually nice-looking man of about sixty, tall and slightly stooped.

"Not in the least," I lied. "What would you like? You name it. We have it."

"Oh, just a sandwich. Whatever's handiest."

I couldn't help laughing. "Whenever a man says that, I know he'd really like a steak with all the trimmings."

In the walk-in, I picked out a particularly elegant T-bone, left it on the serving counter while I put on a fresh pot of coffee and made another quick trip to the walk-in for a fine red tomato and a small bowl of grated potatoes. The stranger watched me with a half smile of approval and I began to feel extremely efficient, putting the potatoes on the back of the grill and being generous with the butter. As soon as they were a crusty brown I turned them over and plopped the steak on a little island of butter on the hot spot. The stranger had told me he liked his steak medium rare. I knew I had to work fast. I set a platter to warm, peeled the tomato and put it on the counter, a knife waiting beside it.

When the man walked over to the kettle sink to wash his hands, I sneakily passed a clove of garlic over the steak and surrounded it with more butter. By the time he turned around there wasn't a sign of garlic anywhere. I was innocently toasting two slices of my homemade bread, which

I cut in two and placed on the platter. Then I turned the steak, added sliced tomato and hashbrowns to the platter, seasoned the steak and lifted it lovingly. It had all taken about four minutes and the man had just dried his hands when I carried the platter triumphantly to the table nearest the kitchen. The stranger dug into the food as if he had not eaten for days.

"Cream?" I asked, bringing in a cup of coffee.

"No thanks. This is great. Do the loggers eat like this all the time?"

"Mister, you've only got a *snack* there. Just an appetizer. You ought to see the way our loggers eat. They're a pretty spoiled bunch. We even given them hot bread every night for supper."

"Well, it's mighty kind of you to go to this extra bother."

"No bother," I told him airily. "You're just as welcome as if you were Mr. Coos Pacific himself."

The man practically choked.

"What's so funny?" I asked.

"I *am* Mr. Coos Pacific," he chuckled. "I thought you knew."

Silently I thanked my lucky stars. I might have taken an instant dislike to the man and served him the skimpiest snack allowed by courtesy and the laws of hospitality. A limp egg, maybe. Burnt toast. Not that he would have had me fired. Still, the reputation of the Ticoma had been at stake and it had come through unblemished.

"Look, Miss er—" he began, still laughing and looking pleased.

"Emmerson. Lee around here."

"Well, I'm glad you help 'spoil' our loggers."

I thanked him and went back to my pies. I guessed he must be here to consult with Old Fox and Camp Push about the sabotage. A sobering thought. It meant problems at the Ticoma were serious enough to engage not only the camp and the Coos Bay office, but to echo all the way up to Portland.

The next afternoon I found myself involved in the affair. Midge, Bonny and I started out to pick autumn leaves for the cookhouse, all wearing blue jeans and tennis shoes, in order to ford the river if we chose.

"One moment! One moment!" Lucien called, hurrying onto the cookhouse porch. "Has Swivelneck left?"

"Oh sure," Bonny called back. "Today's grocery day, isn't it?"

"Oh my God!" Lucien clapped his hand to his forehead. "The coffee! I forgot to put it on the list."

I think I paled a little, too. For a logging camp to run out of coffee is a disaster which no cook could face with equanimity. What disgrace! Oh, poor Lucien!

"He turned off the main road and headed up the Ticoma," Midge volunteered. "I saw him just a second ago."

I surged instantly into action. "Come on," I cried out to the girls. "We can head him off then." We all started hurrying toward the bridge and I shouted back to Lucien, "How many cases do you want?"

"Six," he called after us. "Hurry! Hurry! Hurry!"

Half a mile from camp we came across the parked truck across the river from a small creek which blundered noisily down a slope. A newly graded road ran along its west bank, leading I supposed to the new landing I had been hearing about.

We stopped and considered what to do. Obviously Swivelneck was up to his usual snooping. If he had been willing to herald his approach, he could have forded the river easily at this point and driven straight to the landing instead of sneaking up on foot. If we waited by the car, we might be stuck for an hour or two. Finally we decided to go on to the landing ourselves.

The show was on a benchlike rise, accessible only by the steepening road which pushed its way between house-sized boulders. Before long we could see the sparpole. It had not yet been rigged, but stood starkly bare of cables and guy-lines in the center of the landing. Nor was there any donkey waiting in position on the hillside. The loading, therefore, had not yet begun, but a cutting crew was still at work. A chain saw hummed doggedly and when we drew nearer we could see two men bucking logs at the top of the road.

"Oh gosh," Bonny's whisper was like a little pig's squeal. "It's the Preacher and the Bear."

We all must have felt the same way about the Preacher and the Bear. We did not consult together. We just scurried in a body behind some tall huckleberry bushes, squatting there and peering furtively out. Swivelneck was up there, too. We could see him clambering over a tangled mess of downed trees, some of them already bucked into logs and some still untrimmed, their broken limbs a jumble of green on the ground.

"You sneaking son of a bitch," the Preacher yelled down at him. "What are you here for *now?*"

"To check your scale," Swivelneck yelled back. The chain saw idled while the two men shouted at each other. The Bear was not doing any shouting. He just stood there, scratching his muffin ear.

"We don't need you," the Preacher said. "We gotta scaler. You better scram."

"He said to beat it," the Bear croaked. He took a step toward Swivelneck and then all at once he jumped back and made a grab for his saw. It quickened under his great paw.

"Don't! Hey, wait—" Swivelneck cried and stopped with his mouth open as the huge log hurtled toward him down the hill. For a second he stood seemingly hypnotized. Then he ran two steps in one direction and leaped wildly back again as the plunging log changed its course. When the end of it struck him, it lifted him right off his feet and tossed him to the ground again, before it came to rest against a tangle of downed logs. I could feel Midge gathering herself together to spring up and I thrust my hand against the back of her neck, pressing her back.

"Let's get out of here, you punchy fool," the Preacher shouted. "Nobody's going to believe *this* was an accident. Leave that saw, you stupid ass. Come *on*." He came hopping down the road like a kangaroo with the Bear rolling along after him.

I think we three stopped breathing. We were only about four feet off the road and the pair passed close enough so that we could actually smell their sweat. The Bear was almost blubbering. "I ain't punchy, Ambie," he kept saying. "You tol' de guy to scram and he didn' scram—"

We crouched there until he heard them splashing across the river and then we rushed over to Swivelneck. He lay against a stump where he had been bowled by the log. He was groaning faintly; his face was ashen but he opened his eyes as we reached him.

"No, don't touch me. Run for help. No, not you, Lee. You stay."

"Look, kids," I cautioned, "be careful you don't catch up to those men. And don't run too fast. You'll fall for sure."

"We won't go away," Swivelneck said. I whirled around,

dumbfounded. Humor from Swivelneck and at a time like this! It hurt to look in his anguished face.

"It's my leg," he said as the girls ran off. "I thought I was a goner."

I had to bend closer to hear him. "Can I light a cigarette for you?" I asked and he nodded. When I had put the lighted cigarette in his mouth I shook out the match and, following the tradition of the woods, dug through the layer of moss and fallen needles to bare earth, spat on the match and tamped fresh dirt over it.

"You'd make a logger all right," he said through lips distorted with pain.

I had never expected to feel this sort of sympathy for Swivelneck. It was almost embarrassing.

For a few minutes he lay with his eyes shut. "I suppose the men think I ask for this sort of thing," he said at last. "I know they hate me for being a company man." He opened his eyes and looked straight up into mine. "This is the first good job I've ever had in my whole damn life. I've *got* to hang onto it."

I could not think of an answer. I felt almost relieved when he fainted, but I was scared, too, although his pulse seemed strong enough. I felt sure the Preacher and the Bear must have had a water jug, and I tore up the hill after it, but when I found the water and carried it back to Swivelneck I wondered if it would be humane to revive him. His leg would hurt him terribly. I could see the bone, pearly white, sticking out of the blood which seeped onto his torn levis.

Swivelneck, moaning with pain, came to and I gave him a drink. "I'm afraid it's warm, but here, it will help."

Swivelneck grabbed my hand and hung on tight, as if

he had to have the touch of another human. I left my hand in his.

It seemed to be hours, but it could not have been more than thirty minutes before I heard the Louse struggling up the steep road. Lucien, Snoozy and John Paul were in front, Bonny and Midge riding in back on the mattress they had brought along. Lucien gave Swivelneck a pain pill and we slid him as carefully as we could onto the blanket and eased him into the Louse. The girls and I got in back with him. It took all three of us to keep him on the mattress. John Paul drove carefully, but Swivelneck's face tightened with agony. By the time we reached camp he was blessedly unconscious again.

John Paul had already asked the Fire Warden at the Patrol Station to radio for an ambulance. We did not have too long to wait. As soon as it crossed the bridge, carrying Swivelneck to town, Old Fox drove up in the pickup. When we had told our story he set out again to radio the police, but the Preacher and the Bear had been on their way before Midge and Bonny ever reached camp and, as far as I heard, they were never caught. Somewhere along their route, they must have telephoned to warn the crooked scaler, because he did not return from the Midwest.

The work sheet told the story clearly enough. When Swivelneck was well enough he and Old Fox went over it together. For several weeks, the scaler must have been taking scale from various cutting crews and adding it to that of the Preacher and the Bear, no doubt pocketing a good kickback himself. By averaging the scale, it was possible to come to a pretty good idea of how much had been stolen and the company made restitution to the swindled crew.

With the Preacher and the Bear gone, everybody in camp

relaxed, I among them. "I didn't know I was so worried," I told Edison. We were sitting on the cookhouse steps at the time. "Now I feel like Boygen. You know how nerveless he looks when he stretches and then settles down and starts to purr?"

Edison shook his head a little. "The Preacher and the Bear had a pretty good thing in their deal with the scaler," he said. "Why would they have pulled a bunch of other tricks—sugaring the motors, fooling with the air brakes? It just got the whole camp into an uproar and didn't do them any good."

"Well," I said uncertainly, "Camp Push seemed to think there might be a nut at work—"

"The Bear was punchy, all right. He'd go berserk if he got mad, the way he did when he turned the log loose on Swivelneck. But the skulduggery was planned ahead and worked out carefully. I can't see the Bear doing that."

"Well, thank heaven they're gone," I told him. "They gave me the creeps." Since they were safely out of the way, I launched into a description of the episode on the porch of the Old Homestead.

I did not know Edison could look so mad. "Why the *devil* didn't you tell me?" he demanded.

I was asking myself the same question and the answer I got astounded me. "Why," I said, "it was because of you. I knew you'd light right into that great ex-prizefighter. And I didn't want you to get hurt." I turned around to laugh with Edison at this inanity.

But Edison was not laughing. He looked like a man who has just caught his first glimpse of home after a long voyage.

chapter eleven

IN western Oregon we practically never have to pray for rain, but unless I am very much mistaken, Old Fox and maybe Camp Push, too, were offering up some private prayers during that dry October. The autumn days grew shorter. There was a nip in the air and a chill which crept in with the setting sun. But never a hint of rain. Each morning I would see Old Fox studying the sky and every silly little cloud that passed overhead. His expression kept growing more and more disgruntled.

Everybody in camp knew we were in danger of losing our biggest order, a real whopper, enough to load several Japanese ships due late in October. The logs were already in the river, fine, straight-grained "peelers," used for making plywood. But we needed rain to raise the level of the water before the logs could be run to Coos Bay in time for delivery to the ships.

"Why don't you put on a dance?" I asked Indian Johnny one evening.

"Dance?" Johnny echoed.

I told him I had heard about Indians in Arizona and New Mexico putting on rain dances. "And I hear they're effective, too, every once in a while. You dance and we'll all follow you."

For a moment I believe Indian Johnny thought I was perfectly serious. As a matter of fact, I really was enchanted by the picture which shaped up in my mind. I could see big Indian Johnny dancing a rain dance, with Old Fox on his stocky bowlegs stamping along right behind him and all the others following, Camp Push, the Bull Buck, the loggers and even little old Snoozy and Lucien, all stamping and bending. John Paul would be stripped to the waist, showing off his tattoos. Altogether a splendid sight. Bonny, Midge and I would bring up the rear. Or maybe I would beat on the triangle, making it sound like drums.

Indian Johnny gave a roar of laughter and ended it with a war whoop. "My people never did dance for rain," he said when he had stopped laughing. He took a few shuffling steps, bending down sideways and making a scalping gesture with his right hand and arm. "They danced when they went on the war path. You want the whole camp to go on the war path?"

"It might be better than all this awful waiting," I told him, feeling gloomy again. According to camp gossip, Coos Pacific needed the money from the Japanese order to bid on our winter show, a superb stand of timber near Elk Creek. Edison had driven me down to see that Elk Creek stand one Sunday. There were hundreds of acres of almost level timber land, where the smallest of the trees stood five or six feet in diameter, rising like towering skyscrapers for a hundred feet before the limbs appeared. I still remembered the sound of the muffled wind blowing softly in the tree tops and the tinkling rhythm of a creek as it flowed along. We had passed a young doe with her twin fawns sleeping. Startled by the jeep, she had touched the fawns with her nose and then waited to make sure they bounded safely away before she followed them. It brought a lump to my throat to think of logging so beautiful a forest but, as Edison explained, the timber was ready to cut and the conservation people thought it should be saved from old age and the beetle. Virtually every logging company in the area wanted a chance at it.

When our rain finally came it made a thorough job of it. All day I had kept running to the cookhouse windows, looking up at the darkening sky and the massing of the clouds. The storm broke just before supper with a shooting arrow of light which lit up the cookhouse in an eerie flash, followed instantly by a crash which almost split my eardrums.

I have always been petrified by lightning. Whenever there is a thunderstorm at night I poke my head under a blanket and quail. But this time I ran right out into it as soon as the driving rain began. It pelted me from every direction and I loved it. I could see men swarming out of the bunkhouses, too, slapping each other on the back in jubilation.

All that week it rained. From the window of the Old Homestead I could look out and see the water rolling by, swift and mud colored, fed by all the little creeks leaping down from the hills. The wind blew so hard that the works had to shut down for several days. The woods were a bedlam, the men said. Loose limbs screeched as they tore out of the trees and widow-makers fell all over the place. Even in the cookhouse, above the roar of the wind, we could hear the moaning of the forest. But nobody minded. It meant the rivers would be high enough for the logs to reach tidewater and be rafted for their trip to the bay.

As soon as the wind died down, the men got ready for the splashing. It was set for Tuesday morning. Monday night I was jarred from sleep by a distant rolling rumble. It came again and I sat up alarmed. The rumble did not sound to me like thunder. This had a sharper, more staccato sound. More like blasting, although I could not imagine who would be blasting at that time of the night. I turned on my flashlight. It was eleven o'clock.

When Old Fox and Camp Push came in for breakfast the next morning they looked as if a mule had kicked them in their respective stomachs. Then I heard the sound of the men talking all around the dining room. It was the sound of angry men, something between a growl and a low snarl. Even Boygen was aware of a charged atmosphere. He leaped under the table in the kitchen and crouched there close against the floor, the fur on his neck standing out.

"What on earth?" I asked John Paul when he came after the hot cake refills.

There was no expression at all in John Paul's pale eyes. "Somebody blasted the dam last night," he said.

"What happened to the logs? Were they—"

"The logs are there all right," he said. "But the water isn't."

So Edison had been right. The Preacher and the Bear had not been responsible for all the trouble in camp. There was somebody else, somebody still among us. I could understand the men's rage. I felt it, too, as well as an awful sense of helplessness.

After our morning's work was done, the whole kitchen crew went over to see the damage. The rain had stopped and the air smelled clean and cool as we drove the five and a half miles to the dam. I was dismayed when I saw the low level of the water. After all the rain the water should have been pouring over the dam. Instead, it was pouring through a gaping, splintered hole on the far side of the log-built structure.

The pond formed behind the dam was some four hundred feet wide and almost filled with mink-brown logs, motionless in the sunlight and stretching upriver as far as we could see. Enormous logs they were, too. When logs are hauled on Oregon highways they can only be forty feet in length. But our logs were splashed and rafted to market so they were sawed sixty-four feet long, with an added foot or so, to allow for end damage. The pond was so low that those nearest shore seemed to be resting in mud rather than water.

About twenty men were working frantically to repair the dam while the rest of the crew milled around, swarming all over the catwalk and the banks. They were subdued now, but I could feel an undercurrent of rage in the very way they moved. Across the river Wild Bill and his Cat were bringing up some straight-grained logs about sixteen inches in diameter which I supposed would be used to repair the dam.

When we climbed out of the car Old Fox spotted us and walked over. "It's a mess." He waved an arm toward the other side of the river. "The logs in that whole section will have to be replaced and we'll have to let all the water out of the pond to do it, too. That's the worst of it."

"It'll rain again tomorrow," I said and got a withering glance from Old Fox for my brainless optimism. He grunted and went charging off again.

As we watched, a truck drove up with a load of logs and stopped on the deck alongside a ramp which men called the dump or skids. The ramp was made of sturdy logs laid at a 75° angle leading out into the pond. When the truck driver released the binder chains which held his load of logs on the truck the logs crashed down the skids to shoot up a madcap fountain of water. After they hit the water, a crew of "log jockeys," walking the logs with a nonchalant ease, guided them by pike pole until the ends all pointed toward the dam's gate.

Four log jockeys, better known as river rats, drove up from Greenwood every working day to operate the dam. I saw one of them set the log he stood on to spinning. He had on his big calk boots, but he kept his footing on the spinning log with the practiced grace of a ballet dancer. Showing off a little, because he saw us watching him, I suspected.

We stayed for a few minutes more and I found myself following Old Fox with my eyes. He was all over the place, moving with a violent energy. I would catch sight of his grey head up on the catwalk one minute and the next he would be stamping along the bank or talking to a pair of State Policemen who were looking over the damage. If the Ticoma could not deliver its logs on time, I suspected it would nearly break Old Fox's heart.

By the next day the dam was repaired, but I was wrong about the rain. Indian summer returned with more delightful weather. The mornings were crisp and cool, but the thermometer always climbed to the seventies by noon. Day by day the streams grew smaller. I would have traded all the autumn beauty of the vine maple and dogwood for a good hard downpour.

As the waiting continued, tension increased almost to the snapping point. I could see the strain in every face. It was generally agreed around camp that the skulduggery going on for the past month was the work not of a nut but of some man planted among us by one of the other logging companies.

"They sure as hell aren't doing it for kicks," Bob Botts said one evening. Bob had been sleeping by his donkey for weeks, with a redbone pup, borrowed from a trapper, tied up nearby. The redbone, he believed, would warn him if anyone approached. I had heard all about it from Edison.

"The fool pup," Edison had said, grinning, "goes nuts everytime he smells a bobcat or a skunk. And then Bob thrashes around and struggles out of his sleeping bag. They've got an awful lot of skunks up there, too, so I don't know when Bob gets any sleep."

Bob looked anything but peaked, being a hefty two hundred-pounder, with a pugnacious jaw and an appetite second only to Powderbox Pete's.

"What Old Fox ought to do," Bob Botts said during a coffee session one evening, "is scout around and find out what company has got a lot of logs rafted down there in the bay. He finds out who wants to sell logs to them Japanese marus, he knows right away who wants to louse up our works."

Moonshine Jake said half a dozen companies had logs cold decked around the bay and how the devil could Old Fox pin it on any one of them?

"Oh dear," I said, "and I thought the trouble would all be over when the Preacher and the Bear took off."

"Hell," Bob Botts said, "I knew all the time that was just a private show. The Preacher and the Bear was only out to swindle the other buckers. It wouldn't do them a damn bit of good to sugar the engines. This here guy, he's a trained saboteur and he's deadly."

A few of the men were taking turns guarding the dam at night with a double-barreled twelve-gauge shotgun. Bob offered to let them use the redbone, an offer which was politely declined.

"That's a smart pup," Bob Botts said indignantly. "If everybody hadn't come roaring down there, trampling around like a herd of buffalo when the dam was dynamited, that pup could of picked up the scent and tracked this guy right down. I'll sure as hell use him the nights I guard the dam."

According to Moonshine, Coos Pacific also had a couple of private detectives planted at the Ticoma working on the problem and passing themselves off as loggers. "A couple of these new men. Heck no, I don't know which ones they are. A lot of these new guys are so dumb they couldn't fight their way out of a paper sack. How could I tell which ones are dicks?"

I did not try to spot the private detectives. But I studied faces just the same, wondering which one hid a heart so ruthless he would endanger a truck driver's life for the money paid him by a rival company, shrewd enough to escape detection and skillful enough to pull off the tricks which had plagued us for weeks. A hundred men jostled into the cookhouse twice a day and one of them was a perfect stinker. No doubt he was eating my hot cakes and maybe he dropped around in the evening for coffee. It gave me the shudders to think of it.

I was too preoccupied with these thoughts to notice Bonny the night Wild Bill was to stand guard at the dam. The thought merely passed through my head that Bonny was even more giddy than usual. If I had paid some heed perhaps I could have saved her from the ultimate humiliation. Poor little kid. She told me all about it after waking me at one o'clock the next morning, sobbing hysterically. In fact, I heard the story twice. Once from Bonny, punctuated by her wails and once from Wild Bill, punctuated by expressions of extreme irritation and a few ribald guffaws.

Bonny, it seemed, in her squirrelly little brain, had dreamed up a dandy lark. She had decided to go down and help Wild Bill guard the dam. Somehow she had managed to latch onto a fifth of good bourbon. Since she was only eighteen, she probably had induced one of the men to get it for her in town. She told Midge I wanted her to spend the night in my cabin, making quite a story about it. According to Bonny, I had become extremely nervous as a result of the trouble around camp. She said I was losing sleep, having nervous chills and indeed was on the point of collapse.

When it was dark she got dressed. Bonny had put on several pounds at camp, but she managed to squeeze her plump little rump into her blue jeans, pulled on a black turtleneck sweater and, armed with a flashlight and the hooch, started out.

It was five and a half long miles to the dam and the bottle kept getting heavier and heavier with every mile, but her daydreaming about the romantic possibilities ahead spurred her on. She had decided not to shout out when she arrived but to surprise Wild Bill. Well, Wild Bill was surprised all right. But it was Bonny who received the real shock.

The men had put up a little shelter on the bulkhead which led to the catwalk. It was made of two-by-fours covered with a tarp and gave the guard a good view both of the dam and of the shack housing the motor which operated the dam's gate. The bulkhead rose eight feet above the river's natural bank and was shored up with jagged rocks.

Bonny forgot all about her weariness when she finally approached the dam. To avoid alerting Wild Bill, she turned off her flashlight, got a comb out of her pocket and carefully fixed her hair. She had to turn on the flashlight again for a minute, she said, while she applied fresh lipstick. Then she snapped it off and started slipping up toward the bulkhead and the shelter where she supposed Wild Bill would be.

But Wild Bill was not in the shelter at all. He had gone across the river to scout around and he was on his way back, by way of the catwalk, when he caught sight of the flashlight's gleam. When he saw it go off again, he judged correctly that someone was trying to sneak up on him. He got himself down behind a boulder with his shotgun ready and waited. The moon had gone down, but finally he could make out a dark shadow moving toward the bulkhead.

Bonny was not traveling as quietly as she thought she was, either. She kept crunching along, stumbling over rocks in the dark, dislodging pebbles and so on. If Wild Bill had been a jumpy person he might have blasted away with his shotgun right then and there and heaven knows what would have happened. Instead, he crept cautiously forward and when the moving figure was about four feet away, he made a flying tackle.

"He leaped right on me like a—an *ape*," Bonny sobbed when she told me the story.

"My God," Wild Bill said in his version, "when I felt that soft little rabbit of a girl instead of some tough saboteur I like to have died. She squealed, too, just like a mouse—'eeeEEK.'"

Naturally, she dropped her bottle and it crashed tinkling on the rocks. "Cheez," Wild Bill said, "bourbon on the rocks!"

By that time he had turned on his own flashlight. "For Pete's sake, Bonny!" he roared. "Are you hurt? What on earth are you sneaking up on me for?"

Bonny was practically out of her head with panic. She gathered herself together, jumped up and started running wildly down the road, shrieking as she ran. Wild Bill, of course, took after her.

Bonny told me her pathetic little story after she came sobbing to my door and while I was taking off her torn and bloody clothes. The sharp rocks had cut her badly. "Please let me stay with you tonight," she begged. "Midge wouldn't understand."

I told her she could stay, but to lie still while I went to the cookhouse for hot water and bandages. She stopped crying while I washed and bandaged and got a pair of my pajamas on her. But she wanted to tell the rest of her sad story. When Wild Bill caught up with her, for a minute she had thought everything was going to be all right after all. It was simply *heaven* to have Wild Bill carry her to his car in his strong arms. But he had seemed awfully annoyed.

"He simply *dumped* me in the back seat. Hard. And he never even asked how bad I was hurt. He just drove like blue blazes, muttering all the time about leaving the blamed dam unguarded. And when he got here he practically shoved me out the car and he said, "Now blow." She had begun to wail a little again. "Honestly, Lee, I just can't understand men, can you?"

"Don't be silly, honey, who can?" I said. "Now you go to sleep and don't worry about it tonight."

Long before I got back to sleep, she was snoring softly. In the morning she looked so forlorn, bandaged and black and blue, that I didn't waken her. Instead I told Lucien and Midge a tall tale about her having fallen off the walk on the way to the privy. I also got a little even with Wild Bill by giving him a very knowing wink.

In a few days Bonny was her sunny self again. But I noticed a handsome young choker setter was getting her special good service instead of Wild Bill. She no longer even wanted to talk about our mystery. The fact that the entire camp was tense with worry did not seem to bother her a bit. She had already contributed her best effort and it had not been appreciated. But the rest of the camp did not relax.

The Japanese vessels, we heard, had cleared Honolulu some time before. There had been no further word, but we knew they could not be too far from San Francisco. After that, it would be only a few days before they reached Coos Bay. And still there was no sign of rain.

Old Fox looked as if he had not slept for a week. He would come in for breakfast in the morning, unshaven and blue in the face after a night spent at the dam. He was taking his turn as guard along with the other men. Mr. Coos Pacific showed up again and spent two hours with Old Fox in the office. When they came out, both of them looked very serious. I know Snoozy was asked to try to keep check as much as he could on the comings and goings of the men in the bunkhouses—dormitories they called them now—and to report anything which struck him as unusual.

In the meantime, work in the woods kept up at full blast. In addition to the logs slated for the Japanese marus, we also had to have enough logs in reserve to keep the sawmill in Coos Bay going during any winter storms, when the cutting crew would not be able to work.

Every morning, as soon as I woke up, I would lie still, listening, hoping to hear the soft lisping of rain or a dripping from the roof. I never heard it. The still dawn would change to another bright, crisp day.

Even the water in our swimming pool among the alders and the maples was at a low level. I went swimming there with Midge and Bonny one afternoon but none of us stayed long. The water was too chilly for any prolonged floating about. We just jumped in, squealing, splashed around for a few minutes and scrambled out again, Midge and Bonny heading at once for their cabins and their afternoon naps.

As I was going into the Old Homestead, I saw Edison's jeep pull up in front of the men's dormitory. He had been down at his tree farm for several days and I wondered if it would look too obvious if I went back to the cookhouse. He was sure to go over there for a cup of coffee. As soon as anybody arrived in camp they always headed straight for the pot of coffee we kept ready on the back of the stove.

I decided I could wander in, pretending to look for something I had left there. A magazine maybe, or a book. Then I caught myself up short. I'm a fool, I thought. I don't need an excuse to go to the cookhouse and look for Edison. I've missed the man like the very devil and it's time I told him so, too.

So I dressed in scrambling haste and ran over to the cookhouse. I had no intention of trying to move quietly, but the back door of the cookhouse was open, I was wearing tennis shoes, and apparently there had been no sound to warn of my coming. I was halfway across the kitchen before a man by the pastry board whirled around and I saw it was not Edison but Bob Botts. He had the sugar bin pulled out and he was filling an old tobacco can with sugar. It did not take the sight of the sugar and the tobacco can to warn me what I was up against. His face did that.

As if I were a long distance away I heard my voice, trying to sound casual. "Don't go dipping that filthy thing into my sugar bin. If you want some coffee, help yourself to the sugar with a spoon. Don't go dipping ... dipping...." My voice faded out completely. We stood there and stared straight at each other.

There are certain stages of human emotions when words stop making any sense. In the heights of love or terror or rage some other form of communication takes over and the mind has nothing to do with it. We were both motionless and speechless and yet on some level of consciousness there was a strange awareness between us. I could feel his fright, as great as my own, and an indecision which waited for some signal to tip it one way or another. And then, still from that lower level of consciousness, I could feel his anger flooding up and directing itself straight at me.

I have always heard about people "seeing red" and thought it was only a figure of speech. The shocking thing is that, as we stood there, Bob Botts saw red and I could see the red, too. Quite literally. All at once, his pupils were not black any more. The red shone through them. That was when I moved. Not consciously. Suddenly, I was halfway across the kitchen and sprinting toward the back door, as if I had soared there.

He caught me just before I reached it. He grabbed my arm and twisted me around and I sunk my teeth into the underside of his elbow. "You little bitch," he yelped, jerking free, but I saw he was grinning, as if he felt a certain pleasure now that he was in action. I do not know whether or not he intended to kill me.

We both heard footsteps coming in through the front door at the same moment. I yelled and Botts threw me savagely against the door jamb. As I hit the floor I saw Edison run into the kitchen, a puzzled look on his face which turned instantly to rage when he saw the blood running down my cheek.

He did not ask any questions. He stepped up and let fly a blow which dropped Bob Botts to his knees. But Bob

Botts popped right back up like a jack-in-the-box and kicked Edison on his shins with his calked boot.

I struggled to my feet, thinking, I've got to do something. It isn't fair. Edison hasn't got his calk boots on. They were slugging away at each other by that time and seemed well matched, but I remembered the club Bob Botts had used on Reese-the-Rig and started running around the kitchen looking for a weapon. I grabbed up an iron skillet just as Botts got in a lucky punch and knocked Edison to the floor. I saw Botts give him a great kick and then jump on him with his calk boots. His hands were around Edison's throat when I hurried up and brought the frying pan down on top of Botts's head.

I do not know what I expected, but I was unprepared for the sight of Bob Botts lying on the floor, still as death, the blood seeping through his matted hair.

"My God, I've killed him," I whispered, horrified.

Edison was examining him carefully. "No, he'll be all right. The wound on his head doesn't seem bad. He had it coming to him. Look at the blood all over *your* face!"

"Please get him to a doctor quick. I'm s-scared," I said, through the grey reeling fog which seemed to be encircling me. The next thing I knew I was in my own cot in the Old Homestead and Midge was washing my cut cheek and looking frightened silly.

"What about Botts?" I asked fearfully.

"Oh, that punk's all right. John Paul took him to the hospital. He'd started coming to even before they left."

Just then Edison came in with some bandages in his hand. "I wonder if we ought to take you in to see the doctor," he said in a worried voice, starting to swab and bandage my cheek.

"No, it's nothing," I protested, feeling wonderfully comfortable and fussed over. "I've always wanted a dimple in my cheek."

"Well, all right. But you're going to stay in bed the rest of the day. I'll bring your supper over." He looked pretty battered himself and one eye was almost closed. "What did that punk try to pull, anyway?"

"Oh good heavens," I cried out, sitting bolt upright in bed. "You don't know! Call Old Fox. Get hold of Camp Push. Botts was filling a tobacco can with sugar."

He gave me a startled look and a long whistle. "I'll be back," he said, heading for the door. "I'll get Old Fox. He's at the dam."

"Oh Edison," I called after him. Edison paused and I said, "That redbone pup Botts was telling about—maybe he's tied up in the woods. He'll starve or—"

Edison gave me that slow smile of his which lit up his whole face, bunged eye and all. "You know, I thought about that, too. When the donkey crew comes in I'll tell them to hunt it up and give it back to the trapper." He waved and disappeared.

While he was gone I spent the time analyzing Bob Botts and decided that the money paid him by some rival company had been only half his motive in sabotaging the works. Botts had dropped a pile at poker while Al King was in camp. Then he had lost Midge to Reese-the-Rig and finally the loggers had given him the silent treatment after he hit Reese with a club. Bob Botts, it seemed to me, was sore at the world in general and the Ticoma in particular.

I was sitting up in bed, wearing a pink angora sweater in place of a bed jacket and drinking coffee when Edison came back with Old Fox and Camp Push.

"How're you doing, gal?" Old Fox asked, sitting on the other cot. The concern in his eyes touched me. Camp Push smiled and let himself down onto a powder box while Edison stood at the foot of my cot.

"Just lazy, Boss," I told him and then I launched into the tale of the sugar. I had the time of my life telling it, too, while the three hung on every word.

"He was the guy, all right," Old Fox said when I finished. He and Camp Push glanced at each other and said in unison, "The bastard."

"Are you going to have him arrested?" I asked.

Old Fox shook his head. "I'd certainly like to, but we'd never make it stick. He's guilty as sin, but we haven't got a scrap of proof that would stand up in a law court. He'd claim he just came into the cookhouse after coffee and you got sore and started to bite him."

"For Pete's sake!" Edison exploded.

"Besides," Old Fox went on, "it would be quite an ordeal for you, Lee. We couldn't prove he was hired by another outfit to throw a monkey wrench in the works, either. He'd just sit tight and keep his mouth shut."

But it seemed neither Old Fox nor Camp Push felt he would get off scot-free. As Push said, the word would get around and not a camp in the country would hire him, least of all the company which had been paying him. "They wouldn't dare," Push said. "He'll head right out of the district."

"Unless you want to press assault charges, Lee?" Old Fox said.

"Good heavens no! I'm just glad I didn't kill him."

During the rest of the conversation I sat back, feeling more and more heroic as Old Fox and Camp Push told me how wonderful I'd been.

"Hit him on the head with a frying pan!" Old Fox kept exclaiming. "While we're guarding the dam with a shotgun, why Lee here, she patters up and hits him on the head with a frying pan!" Then he and Push would go off into great roars of laughter.

I tried to point out that Edison had been wonderful, too, that without him I would probably have been very dead by now. But they brushed off Edison's heroic action. In their opinion, for Edison to tackle the big slob was the most natural thing in the world. That's what Edison seemed to think, too. It was the frying pan of mine which bowled them all over.

Finally I said, "I don't think it's so much; in the movies girls are always hitting people over the head with frying pans. It's not a bit unusual."

"Yep," Push said, "but those girls always hit the wrong guy on the head." Then they all three hooted with laughter again.

"What do you suppose he was going to do with the sugar this time?" I asked.

"I know damn well what he'd try to do," Old Fox said. "He'd try to dump it in the motor down at the dam. And he'd have had to work fast, too." He stood up, looking ten years younger than he had for the past few weeks. "The weatherman is forecasting rain for tonight."

chapter twelve

NOBODY thought Bob Botts had an accomplice, but nobody wanted to take a chance on it either. The men and their shotgun continued to guard the dam.

True to the weatherman's prediction, Indian summer gave way to more rain that polished the woods and scented the air. The bosses went around happily measuring each day's rainfall and the gradual rise of creeks and rivers.

"Well," Old Fox said one morning, while he and Camp Push were having coffee with the kitchen crew, "we can't wait any longer. The ships have pulled into San Francisco and they'll be heading up the coast any day. We'll splash tomorrow."

Splash dams are only a memory now. It had long been the contention of sportsmen, commercial fishermen and finally the State Game Commission that havoc caused by the fall run of logs violated the spawning grounds of salmon and trout and disturbed the wild life along the rivers' banks. Oregonians are as jealous of their teeming fish and game as people of another state might be of gold in the hills or oil underground. If splashing threatened the spawning grounds of salmon, the lairs of trout, the haunts of otter, beaver, muskrat and mink, splashing had to stop. In the autumn of '57 when the danger of forest fires was over for the season, the Coos River Boom Company put a reluctant torch to the last two splash dams in Oregon, perhaps in the entire West.

That torch also put an end to an era. And a splendid era it was, too. Nobody can get very excited about the sight of logs being trucked along a highway. Not the sort of excitement we felt at a splashing when the dam's gate was opened and those huge sixty-foot logs went catapulting over the falls to emerge below in tossing fury, hurtling, shoving, booming their way downriver.

All hands and the cook turned out for the show. Not a living thing was left in camp except baby Boygen and the pigs. The kitchen crew, in John Paul's car, drove to a turn-out above the road where we would have a good view. From there we looked straight down on the canyon and the dam, the pond above it and the river below. Quite a different sight from my last glimpse of it. The logs looked the same, a motionless mass of them extending upriver as far as I could see. But the water was high now, crawling up around the trunks of the trees which encircled the shallows. The trees looked at me like dying sentinels, their roots still tenaciously in the mud, slowly losing their battle against the stifling waters.

Men again swarmed over the river bank, but this time everything was festive. Even the sound of the men's voices sounded different. River rats with their pike poles waited along the banks. This was really their show. As soon as the dam was opened, the run would be in their hands.

Finally I spotted Don Jenks, the river foreman who was the star of the drama and knew it. He was the man who operated the dam's gate. Its cables, as big as a man's wrist, were wound on drums powered by a rackety old motor. As Don strode jauntily toward the little rain-darkened shack housing the motor, everybody stopped talking. A moment later I heard the motor sputter and let out my breath with a sigh of relief when it took on a steady droning sound.

The cables, like quivering knives, ripped the water as they tightened. Slowly the gate began to open. Then all at once I heard a great wrenching protest and saw Camp Push, directing Don from the catwalk, duck to one side as the cable nearest the road swung away loose from the gate, barely missing him in its whiplash. He waved frantically to Don to stop the motor.

When the motor died we could hear the roar of the men above the sound of hissing water escaping through the partially open gate.

"Slack! Slack!" Camp Push yelled.

The motor rumbled again, only this time the cable slackened. I leaped out of the car and ran closer. The catwalk was crowded with loggers and river rats, Old Fox in the midst of them, all trying to catch the loose cable.

"It'll be a hell of a job to refasten that cable with water spurting through the dam," one logger was saying, as I reached the bank. "Too bad the gate opened at all." By that time, the men had managed to grab the cable.

I could hear Old Fox swearing at the top of his lungs and then somebody said, "The cable was cut." The word was shouted all along the line: "The cable was half cut through and tore loose from the eye."

It seemed to me everybody along the river bank and on the catwalk was swearing at once. You take a hundred men swearing en masse and the effect is astounding. The loggers seemed to think the accident was the work of Bob Botts, something he had managed to do before the affair in the cookhouse. After listening for a minute or two, I felt quite sure that Botts would indeed leave the district fast. I heard loggers all around me announcing if they ever caught sight of him again, they would chew him into little pieces and spit him out.

Above the hubbub Camp Push shouted, "Get a hook, Jake. Where's that Indian Johnny?"

Johnny came pushing his way toward the catwalk, yelling, "You want me to splice that cable? It's going to take time."

"There's no other way," Push told him. "Clamps won't hold now."

Crowding as close as I dared, I watched, marveling, while Johnny wove the steel strands through the eye of the hook and back into the cable. When the new hook and eye were ready, he fastened the slackened cable and Don once again started the motor. This time the cable held and the huge timbered gate grumbled open.

An avalanche of muddy white foam sucked through the great hole and came boiling out. Released from their prison, the logs converged on the gate as if they were drawn by an invisible magnet and went plunging over the falls. Before long, below the dam there was a wild jumble of logs, turning end over end, battling their way downstream. A log would start slowly for the gate, then as it neared the waterfall it would quicken its pace, poise for a moment with one end out in space and tumble into the vortex below. Sometimes several logs reached the gate at the same time. Churning, swirling and lurching they would topple into the maelstrom, disappear from sight and then bob to the surface again fifty or a hundred feet below the dam to start the race downriver.

Over it all was the most infernal hullabaloo, the shouts of men, the roar of the cataract, the rushing sound of the river and the loud booming of logs as they collided. When about half the logs were through, Camp Push signaled for

Don to close the gate and the cheering men on the catwalk scrambled to be first to reach the bank.

The river rats piled into their jeeps to follow the log run downstream. It was their job to keep each log free and on the move, to shove it back into midstream with their pike poles whenever one was trapped by a jutting rock or root. One hung-up log can cause a log jam, the ogre of a log run. Sometimes a log jam has to be blasted free and that means a big loss from splintered logs.

Once the logs reached tidewater the river rats, walking the floating logs with practiced ease, would guide them into booms. The booms were traps, formed of logs called "boom sticks," secured end to end with boom chains and forming a hollow rectangle with a pointed nose or "peak" to lessen the resistance. The upriver ends of the booms were left open. River rats, with the help of the tide, would fill them with the floating logs and then close and secure the ends. After that, sturdy little river tugs, taking advantage of the ebbing tide, would tow these rafts to the lower bay, ready for mills or ships.

The sight of the logs racing down toward tidewater reminded me of my school days on the lower river, when our school boats had to battle their way through freshets, steering a careful course among bouncing, runaway logs.

Well, I thought, our splashing was over. Now we could all take a deep breath. The men were starting to climb into their cars. I turned and saw Old Fox still standing on the catwalk. Something strange in his attitude caught my attention. His hand was pressed against his chest. At the same moment a logger started to run toward him. He had covered only half the distance when Old Fox whirled and toppled into the seething water below. For an awful moment he disappeared and then, a hundred feet downstream, I saw his hands stretched upward.

Everybody raced down the river bank, with me bringing up the rear. Old Fox was being tossed about like a rag doll. We would see him one moment, flailing his arms in a vain effort to reach the bank and the next instant he would disappear.

I saw Reese-the-Rig kick off his shoes and dive like a seal from the bank, battling his way out in front of Old Fox. There was a great shout from the men as he caught hold of Old Fox's jacket and silence except for the roaring river as Reese towed him to shore. A dozen hands reached out from the bank and dragged them up. Old Fox's face was dead white, but when they turned him over on the sand, a shudder shook him; he groaned and water gushed from his blue lips.

Somebody was sobbing. I did not know who it was until Edison put his arm around my shoulders and said, "Hey, let's not cry now. He's too ornery to drown."

"Yeah," Moonshine Jake said, "if he didn't have to cut his hair like an air force boy, the Rig would have had something better to grab onto than his jacket."

"Quit babbling like a bunch of nitwits and get me home to some dry clothes," Old Fox growled.

"We're not taking you home," Camp Push said. "You're going straight to the hospital. Here, you drive, Wild Bill. You can beat me. It'll be quicker than getting an ambulance." He noticed me in the crowd and said, "Lee, you go along to hold him on the seat."

Behind me I heard somebody say, "You better *anchor* him, if Bill's driving."

Indian Johnny picked up Old Fox as if he were a child and carried him to Wild Bill's car, while I scrambled into the back seat and held his head in my lap. Snoozy ran up with the blankets which were always kept in the back of the Louse.

As he wrapped the blankets around Old Fox he kept muttering, "You old coot, you, you damned old coot." His lined old face was working and his popping eyes were moist.

"Quit clucking around like a broody hen," Old Fox snapped. He looked up into Snoozy's face with eyes which were uncommonly soft. "Good old friend," he said. "You old bastard."

I had ridden with Wild Bill before, but never like this. He drove like hell on wheels. Before long we caught up with the surge of white water which had been released by the dam's opening. As Wild Bill's car hurtled past, I caught a glimpse of the parked jeeps of the river rats. Two of them had carried their light skiff to the water's edge and were rowing furiously toward a log caught on a ledge across the river. The next instant we had drawn ahead of the log run and I could only wait tensely for the first glimpse of the hospital.

Old Fox was dozing fitfully and it seemed to me his color was a little better. At the hospital, after the orderlies had wheeled him to a bed and the nurses took over, I ran to a phone in the lobby to call Mrs. Knowland.

"This is Lee, Hortense," I began and heard her gasp. "Don't be frightened," I rushed on. "Old Fox is all right. He'll be fine, but he got pretty wet, so we thought the doctor should see him."

"Where are you? Speak *up*, girl!"

"At the hospital. Room 38. Do you want Wild Bill to come after you?"

"I'll get there before he can turn around." Hortense

banged down the phone before the words were well out of her mouth.

Although Hortense and Old Fox lived two miles from the hospital, I barely had time to tell Old Fox she was on her way and get back to the lobby before she came panting up the steps. I had always thought of Hortense as invincible, but at that moment, her face was defenseless and when she saw Old Fox, still pale from his experience and groggy from shots, her wonderful brown eyes filled with tears. But she braced herself and marched into the room with a pretty good imitation of her usual vigor.

"Now, old boy," she said, "what on earth have you been up to?" She took his hand in hers.

Old Fox grumbled something about everybody acting like a pack of fussy old women, but on his blue lips was as tender a smile as I had ever seen.

"The trouble with you, Cass," the doctor said, "you think you're 'just as nifty as you were in 1850.' Your heart's a damn sight smarter than you are. It's given you a warning. Man, you're going to slow down if I have to hog-tie you. And don't think I'm not man enough to do it, either." With that remark, the doctor strode out of the room, not looking back.

"Well anyway, baby," Old Fox said, "we got enough logs through to fill that order."

"I knew you would, Casper," Hortense said. "But the doc's right. You've been working and worrying yourself to a frazzle. As soon as you've rested up here for a few days, we're taking off for Hawaii."

I glanced at Wild Bill and we both faded out of the room. When I looked back, Hortense was still holding on to Old Fox's bed. The log run had been a splendid thing. But in my opinion it could not hold a candle to the sight of those two just looking at each other.

chapter thirteen

OLD FOX'S Hawaiian vacation did not last long, less than three weeks, in fact. As Hortense put it: "Some hooligan lassoed me with a rope of flowers and a doggone bee stung my nose. The bump hadn't even gone down when that man of mine decided to catch the next plane back to Portland."

"Now baby," Old Fox said, winking at me, "if I'd stayed another day, you'd have started learning the hula."

Swivelneck was back, too, hobbling around on crutches and acting exactly as ornery as ever. Instead of mellowing him, his unfortunate experience had made him the more eager. He poked his nose into everything, whether it concerned him or not, winced at each dollar spent and fought Lucien, tooth and nail, over every grocery order. It no longer bothered me. To my surprise, I felt quite tolerant toward the man, particularly after Lucien learned how to handle him. Both Meatball and Mr. Sims had dealt with him after their own fashion, Meatball by digging in his heels and refusing to be intimidated and Mr. Sims by sharpening knives in sinister fashion. Lucien, on the other hand, used psychology and we had peace in the cookhouse.

On every grocery order, Lucien would ring in a joker, some extravagant and totally unnecessary item—a case of imported pâté de foie gras, for example, or ten jars of Romanoff caviar (green seal beluga). Naturally Swivelneck would hit the ceiling. Lucien would then give an impassioned little speech on the necessity for occasional luxuries to add zest to a menu and only after several minutes of violent argument would he allow himself to be talked down. Pleased at his own astuteness and at the saving of company funds, Swivelneck would then let the rest of the list go through without question. This kept Swivelneck in a pleasant mood and Lucien enjoyed the exercise in ingenuity.

He would settle down at the little table in the kitchen and busy himself writing out his order. When I looked over his shoulder he would glance up, cock a wispy eyebrow and write out a large order for truffles, perhaps, or marrons glacés.

"This," he would say, "the good Swivelneck will be sure to appreciate."

"But what would you do if Swivelneck slipped up and actually *bought* all those truffles?" I asked him once. "The loggers would die if you served them truffles."

"We would manage," he said. He stared dreamily into space. "Ah yes," he said with a sigh. "We would manage very nicely."

Poor Lucien. He was never a lucky man. On the one day when he might have extended himself to the utmost, he was away from camp. Lucien seldom took a weekend off, but on this occasion he had decided to go to town, driving in with Midge and leaving me to handle the supper, since it was Friday and we expected only a handful of men.

John Paul, Bonny and I were finishing up the noon work and I was wondering to myself what sort of wild oats Lucien would sow in town, when Camp Push came looking for him.

He seemed a little taken aback at his absence. "Didn't Old Fox tell you we're going to work tomorrow?"

"Oh no," I wailed. "Not the whole crew?"

Camp Push put on the firm expression he always used when he was springing unpleasant news. "Nobody gets paid until tomorrow night," he said. "Sorry, but we're setting up our winter show at Elk Creek. The good weather can't last."

So there would be a hundred men for dinner, darn it. This in itself was no particular catastrophe. I had just grown lazy since Lucien arrived and dreaded the thought of the scramble and rush it entailed.

As I settled down for my afternoon nap, I planned out the menu, the easiest one I could think of. I decided to have veal roasts, and cold plates of canned Chinook salmon garnished with cucumbers, for those who would not eat meat on Fridays. I had baked fresh bread that morning; the girls had peeled a sack of spuds and there was plenty of pastry. The job would not be too hard. All the same, I was annoyed. I was also sick and tired of logging camps, I decided, where you plan supper for six and find you have a hundred men to feed. Such things simply don't happen in a family situation. I remembered my nice fat bank account. I could go back to Ole and El's, settle down to writing and have money enough to pay room and board for a good long time. But what about Edison?

Well, what about him? I asked myself. I always shied away from thinking about Edison right through to a conclusion. I certainly hoped it was not because of any lingering memory of Doug. I hoped I was not that much of a fool.

Edison was planning to build at his tree farm during the winter and I knew I was included in his plans. The thought of Edison was never very far away from me. But it kept on being such a *vague* thought, as if I simply did not want to grapple with it.

A knock on my door startled me. I pulled my robe closer and called "Come in," without bothering to get up.

Old Fox opened the door. He looked embarrassed. For a moment I thought he was going to object to my resting so early in the afternoon, so I bristled.

"Look, Lee," he began, "this isn't my idea at all."

"What isn't?"

"Well, the home office. It's their idea," he mumbled. "I didn't have a thing to do with it."

I began to get exasperated. "Old Fox will you *please* look at me? What are you trying to say?"

"Well," he said apologetically, "the main office has invited the Timber and Soil Conservation bunch up here for dinner at five."

"Tonight!" I yelped, sitting up in bed.

"Yep, tonight. I hate to tell you, but there's about twenty-five of them. About half the millionaires in the state, I guess. There's one of the Weyerhaeusers and the heads of Menasha and of Evans, to mention a few of them. Also our own big bosses. Oh yes, and half a dozen leading farmers."

I fell back and closed my eyes.

"I tried all over town to find Lucien, but no luck," Old Fox went on, while I lay as one dead. "I hate to do this to you, Lee."

I opened my eyes and gave him a cold stare.

"But I brought choice T-bones and fresh crabmeat for cocktails," he said brightly, as if that made everything all right.

"Oh dandy," I groaned. "So now poor John Paul has to cut steaks for the whole crew."

"What?"

"Look, you've been around logging camps all your life. You know perfectly well we can't feed steaks at five to our guests and roast veal to the crew at six."

"Oh," Old Fox said. He squirmed around for a minute and then asked weakly, "Is there anything I can do to help?"

"Just scram and let me lie still and collect my wits for fifteen minutes. Then I'll go and break the news to John Paul. I hope poor Bonny is getting her nap."

Old Fox left practically on tippy-toes.

I have often read stories in which some stupid husband brings the boss home to dinner with insufficient warning to his wife. This is always enough to send the poor wife into a tailspin. And rightly so. Sometimes the marriage itself is endangered. But suppose *twenty-five* big important people suddenly arrived. What would she do then? Particularly if she had to produce another dinner for a hundred men only an hour later? I know what I did. I lay on my bed and groveled in panic and self-pity. That is, until I started planning what to serve. Then, all at once, I experienced a little quiver of excitement and pleasure. This was drama and I do love drama.

Well, I thought, steaks for the guests and steaks for the crew, plus the salmon platters. So far, so good. For the guests, we would start off with the crabmeat cocktails, in Lucien's superb sauce left over from Wednesday. We'd have to save out enough crab to put into the crew's salad, at least a token amount, to appease them in case they got wind of the guests' cocktails. For the guests, tossed green salad, made by John Paul.

For a moment I considered knocking out the eyes of the guests with Lucien's potato volcano and then sternly forced my mind into more practical channels. No potato volcano.

No chocolate soufflé. I would play it cool and safe. I would serve French bakes and apple pie for dessert. A pie is always safe and we had plenty. I knew where Lucien had squirreled away some aged Tillamook cheese, too.

Since we had to have two ovens for the crew's spuds, I could not make hot bread. Anyway, I thought a little smugly, my homemade bread is better than biscuits and if the crew runs out and has to finish with bakery bread, for once, it won't kill them, the spoiled brats.

After pondering a moment, I made up my mind to swipe some of Lucien's mushrooms for the peas. He would have a fit, if he knew, but I could ask Old Fox to bring up some more mushrooms the next day and probably Lucien would never find out. Then I made a bold decision. I would also swipe some of his special fig preserves. Daring, I knew, but I would have dared anything that day.

The meal seemed badly in need of a creamed dish. Creamed onions, I thought, with lots of butter and a crumb topping. Three casseroles would do it. Bonny would not have time to peel onions for the crew, too. Instead, I would give the crew beans. The loggers would always settle for beans. I could open three of the gallon cans Mr. Sims had ordered, put in some chili sauce, a hint of garlic, cover them with cheese and bake them after the guests' spuds were out of the oven. The crew would never suspect the beans of being relics from Mr. Sims's sojourn.

For the loggers, ice cream and cookies for dessert, since they had guzzled apple pie for lunch.

Well, I thought, we have it cooled. I leaped up, scrambled into my dress and hurried over to warn Bonny of the emergency we had to face. Bonny was almost always good natured and on this day, when I spoke of tycoons and lumber barons, she looked positively elated.

"Man, oh man," she squealed, heading immediately for her powder-box dresser and the mascara.

"Oh *not* mascara, Bonny," I cried out. "Oh, please."

Bonny thrust out her lower lip, looked stubborn and opened jars, while the most frightful picture formed itself in my mind. I could see Bonny going hog wild, rattling around the cookhouse, jingling bracelets and earrings, giggling hysterically and finally spilling creamed onions over the head of Mr. Coos Pacific.

In this emergency, I remembered Lucien and psychology. "Old Fox is so proud of you," I said. "He'll want to show you off to all those men and it will break his heart if you don't look lovely and dainty, the way you usually do."

Bonny paused, with a dreamy expression in her eyes. "Just a *little* mascara?"

"No," I told her. "None. No earrings, either. But wear that pretty blue linen dress, the one Camp Push admires so...." I hurried out of her cabin, hoping for the best, leaving her standing there, obviously torn between two conflicting pictures in her own mind—Bonny, the exotic beauty, and Bonny, the perfect flunkey.

John Paul caused no trouble at all. I knew he wouldn't. He just shrugged his shoulders and went about cutting steaks for the loggers' supper from a hind quarter of beef marked choice.

By four thirty the greater part of the battle was won. The cocktails were on a tray in the walk-in being chilled. Bread was sliced and wrapped in clean dishtowels. The peas and mushrooms were ready to put on the stove and the onions were crumb topped, waiting for the oven where the French bakes were already growing golden. The crew's dinner was also ready for the final stages and the guests'

T-bones were on the serving table, so they would be at room temperature when I started to fry them at the last minute.

Three tables were set up with an extra place at each table in case Old Fox had counted wrong—which he had. Twenty-six guests, not twenty-five, finally arrived.

Bonny looked perfectly charming, hair shining, face clean. But she *was* giggling a little hysterically, I noticed with alarm.

"Gosh, Lee," she said, "aren't you going to pretty up at *all?* Your nose is awful shiny and your dress is all wet and horrid looking across your shoulders and your—"

"Oh heavens! I'd forgotten," I cried. "Look, you watch things. I'll be back in a minute."

I rushed over to the Old Homestead, doused myself with cold water, hurriedly repaired my face, combed my hair, got into my newest dress, a nice lavender cotton, and then ran back to the cookhouse again, and began frying steaks. I had to guess at the degree of rareness and settled on the likeliest combination—six well done, eleven medium, six medium rare and three rare.

Above the noise of the frying, I could hear the guests arriving. A quick glance assured me Old Fox was seating them while Bonny put the crab cocktails on the tables. She was not giggling, either. She was moving about most unobtrusively. "Okay, we're ready," John Paul said in a few minutes and I dished up the hot food, while Bonny took away the empty cocktail glasses.

When she carried in the platters, I heard Old Fox say to our guests, "You'll have to pass the food along the table. Our butler just stepped out."

At last I had a moment to glance at our guests. Oh golly, I thought, beginning to feel a delayed fright. All the big bosses, all the big shots in the industry. What a disgrace for Coos Pacific if I've forgotten to salt the onions—but no, clearly nothing was seriously wrong. They were attacking the food with great eagerness. Or was that thin man only picking? No, it was all right. He had just taken an enormous mouthful. I think I felt a little like a prima donna. There is something uniquely satisfying about seeing people eat the food you've cooked. I had always felt a curious pleasure when the frantic hurrying was over and the crew lit into their supper with gusto. This time the pleasure was magnified, probably because of the intensity which had preceded it.

Then all at once my complacency was shattered. Completely and utterly. A tall man on the number two table glanced up and I found myself looking straight into the face of Doug Weatherby. He smiled at me airily and quirked a humorous eyebrow. I hope I shut my mouth which must have dropped open. I know I backed away from the serving table and tried to steady myself.

Bonny was talking but her voice came to me from a long distance away. "Boy, are they eating! Talk about our loggers! They're sure bragging about the cook, too."

"You all helped," I said mechanically, my mind almost a total blank. Only a few jumpy thoughts whirled around there, a wonder at his being here at all, a sickening sense of embarrassment at his finding me cooking in a logging camp—of all corny things to be doing, when I was supposed to be so literary and everything—oh hell. And the trouble was, he was even handsomer than I remembered. And damn him anyway, quirking his eyebrow and looking so amused.

I stood with my back to the dining room, automatically refilling the dishes John Paul and Bonny brought to me.

Well, at last it was over and with relief I heard them leave.

But there was no chance to collect myself. We all had to pitch in and reset the three tables. After that it was time to fry the loggers' steaks. When the men started their supper, pleased and surprised at having steaks on Friday night, I went out onto the back porch to try to cool my head. There should not be any empty platters for a few minutes anyway.

What I felt at the moment was a terrible dejection. All the things which had made me proud during the summer were silly things, I could see now. Hitting people over the head with frying pans, biting men in the arm. These were not things to be proud of. They were simply undignified and I shouldn't have got myself into such messes in the first place. Feeding a hundred loggers was not an accomplishment to brag about either. Seen through Doug's eyes, it would just be menial. He probably would be ashamed to admit to his friends that he even knew a second cook in a logging camp. Or maybe he would make a very funny story about it to his wife.

Just then Doug walked around the corner of the cookhouse, with another man.

"Mr. Knowland told me I'd find you here," he said, smiling widely. He did not look ashamed of knowing me. In fact, he looked as if he were going to kiss me and when I forestalled him by thrusting out my hand, he put on rather a wry expression. Unquestionably there was a caress in his eyes.

"How did *you* ever get so far from civilization?" I asked, hoping he would not see how my knees were shaking. I turned to smile at the man with him. "Why, Chuck Marsh! I haven't seen you for a hundred years."

"How goes the battle with you, Lee?" Chuck said.

"I haven't been in any plays lately."

Chuck laughed and said to Doug, "We had the leads in our class play. I got to enfold her in my arms at the finale."

"And all the kids said I fell against you like a ton of bricks."

"She's improved," Doug said. It certainly sounded to me as if his voice held a possessive note. "The Elks Club has a shindig tomorrow night. How about going to the dance with Chuck and his wife and me?"

"And your wife?"

He raised his shoulders a little and let them drop again in a gesture which I could not interpret exactly. "I haven't got one."

Right then my ears began to ring. I wanted to dance. I wanted to yell. Instead, I think I managed to look unconcerned. After shrugging away the question of wife and holy matrimony, he went on about how he and Chuck had been roommates at the University of California. He said he had learned my address from El, remembered his friend Chuck, who lived in Coos Bay, wangled an invitation to go elk hunting and here he was.

Bonny came out on the porch and said, "Lee, I'm sorry. I need more steaks."

"Be right there," I told her. I looked at Doug. The man had always been able to melt me with a smile. "Well," I said, still trying to be a little aloof, "if you want to pick me up at eight tomorrow night, okay, if you'll bring me back here after the dance. I have to get Sunday breakfast."

I wandered through the next day in a state of shock. In the evening, when I had put on the jade and blue evening gown and the fake fingernails, my image came rippled and twisted back to me from the cockeyed mirror in the Old

Homestead. All the same it was a blue and jade and golden image and it could not discourage me. Not that night.

I had splurged on the dress in San Francisco, hoping to impress Doug with it. He had never been around after that to impress, but Saturday night it lived up to its destiny. When Doug called for me at eight, he looked me over with decided approval.

"Well, what did you expect?" I demanded out of some miserable residue of resentment. "Did you expect me to wear my cook's apron?"

"Not at all," he said a little coldly. "But I'd forgotten how you *could* look."

That mollified me. As he drove downriver, I settled back in the car and felt exactly as if I were sliding down a moonbeam. He did not say a word about that other girl, why he had become engaged to her or why he was not engaged to her any more. Nor did I ask him, because at the moment I did not want to share my moonbeam with even the shadow of another girl.

While he gave a hilarious account of the day's hunt (no elk) and described visits in San Francisco with Ole and El, I tried to get used to the stupefying idea that sometimes everything *does* come out right in the end.

Chuck's wife turned out to be a girl I had gone to school with. I liked her. I liked everything. We danced all night and by the time Doug pulled up in front of the Old Homestead, it was five thirty in the morning, only an hour before I had to start late Sunday breakfast.

Doug would not stay for breakfast. He said all he wanted was some sleep, but I think I surprised him when I gave him a quick kiss, jumped out of the car and admonished him to stay awake and not run into the river. I certainly was not going to sit in the car with him when all the yard lights were on. Not in a logging camp, I wasn't.

I had no time even for a catnap. I took off my dress, my high-heeled slippers and my fingernails, got into a workday outfit and set out for the cookhouse. Not the slightest wind was stirring. The dawn was so silent it seemed to be holding its breath. So was I. Dreams and reality were mixed up in the most confusing way. They were all one. Doug had insisted that I marry him. Imagine that. *Insisted*. Doug, who had never breathed a word about marriage to me before. He wanted me to drive back to San Francisco with him. His own prospects for the future looked brighter than ever, too. When I knew him he had been having something of a struggle with his small contracting business. But he had picked up some undeveloped property in California, had managed to interest big money in a country estates development and now he was on his way to big things.

Big things, I thought, and found myself looking hard at my two chubby thumbs, something I had not done for months. The truth was, all at once I felt unsure of myself again and absolutely inadequate to the new plans. Nonsense, I told myself, I will make Doug a perfect wife. He can bring twenty-six big important people home to dinner at the last minute and I will know exactly how to handle the situation.

chapter fourteen

DOUG and Chuck Marsh were going on a hunting trip, packing in to the headwaters of the west Millicoma, so I had a week to adjust my mind to the metamorphosis from camp cook to Doug's future bride. It took some doing. The coming-true of an impossible hope can be a disconcerting experience, I discovered.

All week I avoided being alone with Edison. I delayed telling him about Doug because I could not quite bring myself to believe in the reality of my plans. I would find myself thinking, in fright, I'll bet Doug never does come back here after the hunting trip. I'll bet he was only kidding. A nonsensical idea, no doubt, but it plagued me just the same. So did the puzzled look in Edison's eyes.

The main excitement in the cookhouse during that week revolved around the Friday evening shower and party we were giving Midge and Reese-the-Rig, who were going to be married soon. The loggers had taken up a collection to which even Swivelneck had contributed a dollar or two. When Bonny and I went into town for the shopping, we had $296 to spend. After splurging on a toaster, iron, waffle iron, electric frying pan, mixer and a starter set of silver, we had enough left for some linens and beautiful Pendleton blankets.

Lucien baked a cake as big as a washtub and decorated it with pink and white rosebuds, hearts, cupids and doves, while Bonny and I made quantities of ridiculous little sandwiches to give the loggers a laugh. Under Lucien's direction, we made a punch of canned fruit juice, oranges, lemons, and ginger ale, a mildly pleasant concoction which turned into something rich and strange when Moonshine Jake sneaked a couple of jugs of moonshine into it. But at least it served to get the party off to a rollicking start.

The celebrating began as soon as we had cleared away the supper dishes.

After Midge had opened her presents and Reese-the-Rig had cut the first slice of cake rather messily with a new topping saw which somebody produced for the occasion, we pushed the tables back against the dining-room wall and danced. Snoozy played the harmonica, Indian Johnny the guitar and Midge, Bonny and I were danced off our feet. The rest of the crew linked arms and circled boisterously around, stomping, singing and generally raising hell. I do not believe I danced more than a minute with any one partner before some other logger would come cutting in. It was the same with Midge and Bonny. There were loggers who stomped and loggers who glided and loggers who had swallowed too much punch and howled when they danced. I not only felt wildly popular, I also felt a little like a volleyball shot along from hand to hand.

In the midst of the wild uproar, John Paul brought word that someone was asking for me at the door. I knew it would have to be Doug, back from hunting sooner than I had expected. So he had not taken a powder. I felt weak with relief at the sight of him, standing there, lean, handsome and perfectly wonderful. I also felt flustered. Being leery of the punch, I had drunk sparingly, but I knew my face was flushed and my hair ruffled. No wonder, either.

"Sorry to come so late," Doug said, "but I shot my first elk today."

"Wonderful! How many points?" I asked, hurriedly trying to smooth my hair and getting into a panic. I suspected he might want to start south right away. Maybe tomorrow.

"A five-pointer at two hundred yards," he said. "Get your coat, hon. You're going to spend the rest of your weekend at Chuck's."

I stammered out something about being one of the hostesses at the party and unable to leave yet. Finally I inveigled him into the cookhouse with the offer of some real, unadulterated logging-camp punch. He made a face when he first tasted it, then looked mildly surprised and held his glass out for a refill.

After we danced a few times around the room, he steered me to the punchbowl again and I introduced him to Midge, Bonny and their partners. I think Doug could have charmed the fleas right off a dog's back. Both girls looked flattered every time he smiled at them and, when he emptied his cup and danced away with Bonny, she was virtually glassy eyed with admiration.

I had gone only a few feet with Bonny's partner before Edison cut in. And now's the time to tell him, I thought, or at least sort of hint. But before I could open my mouth Moonshine Jake whirled me away from Edison. Moonshine was barely able to navigate by that time. He was followed, in rapid succession, by Reese-the-Rig, who circled the room at an alarming speed, and Doug again, growing quite insistent now about my leaving—leaving the camp for good and all, right then.

"But I've simply got to give Old Fox two weeks' notice," I told him as we headed toward the punchbowl.

A young whistle punk was singing at the time. He was

dancing with Midge, holding her as close as he could and, in a haunting tenor, crooning something about being in love, "while I dance, dear, with you."

Reese-the-Rig, who stood near us at the punchbowl, immediately went into a slow burn. I could see his big fists clenching and unclenching. "For heaven's sake," I whispered to Doug, "quick, cut in on that singer. Reese is about to blow his top and we can't have a fight now."

"A loggers' fight? Swell," Doug said with satisfaction. "This I've got to see." Then rather an odd, intent look came over his face as I caught Edison's eye and rolled my own meaningfully toward Midge and the whistle punk. Edison got my message and cut in on the pair, to Reese's obvious relief. Reese gulped his drink and cut in on Edison. I noticed that during this byplay, Doug kept watching me with both eyebrows cocked and a one-sided grin on his face.

"Whom were you going to give two weeks' notice to?" he asked. "Old Fox? Or somebody else maybe?"

So the man was jealous! The knowledge delighted me. It never hurt anybody to be a little jealous, I thought. But the time had come when I had to talk to Edison, I realized, right now, before I gave notice to Old Fox.

As it turned out there was no need to tell Edison. When the party was over he followed me to the walk-in as I carried back a pitcher of cream. "You're going back to San Francisco with him, aren't you," he said, making it not a question but a plain statement of fact.

"Not until I see Old Fox and give two weeks' notice," I said. I wanted to add, "I'm sorry," but you don't offer sympathy to a man as dignified as Edison was as he stood there, holding the refrigerator door open for me.

"Be happy, Lee," he said. "Good night, now." He walked

out the back door and when it closed behind him, I stood staring at it, wanting to cry.

It was late when Doug and I reached the Marsh's and terribly late when I got up Saturday morning, to the bliss of a soak in a full-length tub and a lovely leisurely breakfast. Doug was wonderfully attentive. He even got my breakfast for me, since Chuck and his wife had already gone into town. I knocked myself out trying to be attractive. I hung on his words and laughed uproariously at every one of his quips. Oh dear, I thought, maybe I'm laughing *too* much. I'm getting a little hoarse. But I simply could not stop myself from being vivacious all over the place, and Doug certainly seemed to appreciate it.

At one point I stopped long enough to say, "You know, you look different somehow."

"How do you mean?"

I studied him carefully and with some surprise, although I could not decide exactly where the difference lay. "I don't know. Just a little different."

"Getting old looking or something?" he asked, obviously not too pleased. "Notice any grey hairs? A paunch forming? Signs of senility?"

"Oh my no," I cried and then I blundered around and said, "More distinguished," which really wasn't what I meant at all.

"Possibly more successful," Doug said, in good humor again. "I can spot it six feet away when a man's on the way up."

Chuck and his wife had a bridge date for the evening, but Doug said we could go to the Elks Club to dance again, if I felt like it, since Chuck had given him a guest card. In the meantime, since he was pretty well bushed after his week's camping trip, he settled down for an afternoon nap and I hurried into town to buy a new evening dress, the most extravagant one I could find, as well as an extraordinary array of beauty aids and perfume. Morale boosters. These I needed badly to help me lick the horrid old sense of inadequacy which I felt whenever I was with Doug.

Chuck and his wife were home having a drink with Doug in the family room when I got back. I flopped into a chair, packages strewn all around me. "It's easier to cook for a hundred men than buy one dress," I said, as Chuck handed me a glass.

"And she still wants to keep on cooking," Doug said. "Won't leave for two weeks." He was sitting on a davenport, long legs stretched out in front of him, feet crossed and a devilish look about him. "She can't bear to leave all her wonderful friends, if you ask me."

"Nobody did," Chuck said under his breath, but I don't think anyone else heard him.

Doug got up. He chose an olive from the tray of hors d'oeuvres, shoved it under his lower lip and walked several paces all humped over, with one hand on his back. "O-oh, oh," he said in a quavering falsetto, "my lumbago is nigh killing me."

Everybody laughed, I louder than anyone. It was a clever takeoff on Snoozy, but I felt a little uncomfortable for laughing, just the same.

Doug ran his hands through his hair in an attempt to make it stand straight up. He planted his feet firmly apart and looked stern. "Sorry, gentlemen," he said in a whip-cracking voice, "but our butler just stepped out."

My laughter was weak that time. At camp, we had often kidded about Snoozy and even Old Fox. But we did it with affection. Doug made them seem grotesque. Or maybe I was being super sensitive and still had a chip on my shoulder. In any case, I found myself growing tense, waiting for the next takeoff. Fortunately there were no more, since one of the children yelled, just then, waking from his nap and creating enough disturbance to break up the party.

Doug took me to a Chinese restaurant for dinner. Our date started out to be fun, but it deteriorated faster than dead fish left too long in the sun. Doug had been talking about his big business deal and I was suitably impressed by the way he had handled the financing. But he went on and on, into what seemed to me quite unsavory details, all about an illiterate old alien who had lived alone for thirty-five years on the forty acres Doug wanted, refusing to sell. Doug found out that the old man's papers were not in order and had been able to get the deportation ball rolling.

I swallowed a fried shrimp and said, "Oh dear, wasn't he awfully unhappy?"

Doug looked at me as if I had suddenly flipped. "He was breaking a law, wasn't he?" he asked in disgust.

Well, laws are laws and I approve of them. But I did not approve of Doug's looking so triumphant about it. I even had a horrible suspicion that he had enjoyed the affair.

"Anyway," he said, "it was time the old geezer went back to the fatherland and got buried with his ancestors."

I dragged along over to the Elks in a depressed mood. Doug, I knew, had saved the choicest lot in the development for our own house. At the moment the idea did not invigorate me a bit.

One thing I had always known about Doug. Whenever he drank a little too much, he got silly. Being in Oregon, we could not buy liquor by the drink. We had to bring our own bottle. With some uneasiness, I noticed Doug giving two bottles to the bartender, so there was no hope of running out. We danced a lot, but he drank even more and the more he drank, the more awkward I seemed to get. Twice he stepped on my toes. Automatically I said, "Sorry," and he smiled an acceptance of my apology.

Between dances, as we sat in a secluded corner, he was most attentive. Unfortunately, a timber cruiser, whom I knew slightly, left his coat and hat on a nearby chair when he got up to dance and Doug grabbed them. He put them on and threw out his chest.

"For heaven's sake, don't be so silly," I begged him, but he dragged me out onto the dance floor.

"Don't I look like that logger you're so keen about, hon? Ain't I the devil of a looker in this rig?"

I don't know whom he thought he was taking off that time. He certainly did not look a bit like Edison. In fact he looked ridiculous. "Well, you don't dance like him," I said, managing to free myself and get back to the table. Luckily the timber cruiser recognized me. When I gave him back the hat and coat, stammering apologies, he was good natured about it. But I caught a sardonic expression in his eye when he glanced at Doug. Men seem to save that particular expression for other men whom they consider too awful even to get mad at.

Doug however was extremely pleased with himself. And what on earth is happening to *me?* I wondered. My teeth were on edge and I was ready to scream. This guy, I thought with a terrible clarity, is a perfect *ass*.

I leaned back, dumbfounded. Doug, I remembered, had looked different to me when I studied his face that morning at breakfast, as if he had changed in some way. Well, he had not changed at all. I was the one who had changed.

"What's that logging boy friend's name, anyway?" Doug asked.

"Edison," I said automatically. A whole sheaf of pictures

came tumbling into my mind, like cards from an IBM machine. Edison walking past me in Golden Gate Park, Edison when he charged on Bob Botts and the way he looked standing by the fir at his tree farm. I seemed to see each picture much more clearly than I ever had seen Edison in real life. I never had seen him at all before, except through a shadow cast by this Doug Weatherby.

"El told me she was afraid you were falling for some lout up here," Doug said. "That's one reason I came right up."

"No she didn't," I told him. "El didn't say 'lout.' That was your idea. And don't you say it either, because you're talking about the man I'm going to marry." My voice was shaking and I knew I sounded ridiculously melodramatic. For some cruel reason, whenever I say anything I feel very intensely it comes out sounding like a soap opera. That night I did not give a damn. I snatched my bag and jumped up, too mad to say another word. Doug started to get up, too, looking startled, but he settled back again at once and grinned. He thought this was all part of the game. He knew I would come back soon, subdued.

But he was wrong. I did not even phone for a taxi, although it was raining. I ran all the long blocks to the taxi stand. When I told the fat cab driver I wanted to go to the Ticoma camp, his red face peered out at me suspiciously, the same driver who had been at the stand when I first arrived in Coos Bay, looking for a job. I remembered his saying, "Nobody takes a cab up there, lady, but a bunch of drunken loggers."

"Yes," I said, "I know it will cost me thirty dollars." I climbed in and collapsed against the cushions. I wasn't drunk, but all right, dammit, I *was* a logger. And I was also free as a bird. After enjoying this sensation for a few minutes, I thanked whatever lucky star had brought Doug Weatherby up to Oregon. I might have gone on for months and months, carrying the torch. The rest of the trip I spent deciding what I could say to straighten things out with Edison.

I got up early Sunday morning and hurried to get breakfast, in hopes that Edison might not have gone to his tree farm for the weekend after all. Bonny met me in the kitchen. "What on earth are you doing here today?" she asked.

"I got homesick," I told her shortly, so shortly that Bonny looked hurt and a little put out.

She slanted her eyes at me and said huffily, "I suppose you've heard Edison Smith quit his job. He's not coming back anymore."

chapter fifteen

AS frequently happens in Oregon, the rain forgot to stop. Day after dreary day it came pelting down, drove the color from the woods and turned mounds of bright leaves to sodden, doleful brown. I felt every bit as sodden and doleful. Finally I buttonholed Wild Bill and asked him if Edison was at his tree farm.

The glint in Wild Bill's green eyes was by no means as friendly as usual. I only caught the one glint before he looked away, over the top of my head, refusing to be led into any talk about Edison. Sounding stiff and aloof, he said he did not know where Edison was. He only knew he had quit his job for good. His final remark, as he strolled away, staggered me. "He may have gone back to Minnesota," he said.

Still the rain came down, without letting up for an instant, until at last all logging was suspended and every logger, who had a place to stay, left camp. Midge already had gone home to make her wedding arrangements and finally John Paul, too, told me good-bye. He was going back to sea.

I fumbled around in my mind, trying to think of something to say to this remote and self-contained man beyond the usual, "Good luck," or "I hope we meet again." I wanted to cry out, "Are you unhappy, John Paul?" and maybe weep a little bit with him about life and love and loss. But, looking up into his shuttered face, I could only manage: "It was a strange summer, John Paul."

As usual, John Paul seemed to be on the very verge of making some profound and astonishing remark. Instead he said, "It's the woods. The woods does something to women."

And I did not know *what* to make of that.

He left in the middle of a terrible downpour. I stood in the cookhouse door to wave him off. He had wrapped his Coca-Cola ad in a piece of tarpaulin and strapped it to the roof of his car. Maybe it still meant Gina to him, or maybe once again it was his lucky lady and Gina only a faint and almost painless memory.

Lots of other men had started off alone, since I had been in camp, but none of them gave the same impression of solitude as John Paul when he drove away down the road. I could imagine him in so many places, on all the seven seas and all the ports of the world—Marseilles, Naples, Tahiti—always alone and probably hearing the laughter of his dead Agnes in every gull's cry.

It rained for two weeks. Only Lucien, Bonny and I were left of the kitchen crew and we were feeding only half a dozen men. I spent hours in the Old Homestead, hearing the monotonous slop of raindrops on my shake roof and trying to compose a letter to Edison. My long-winded explanations sounded so absurd that I crumpled the letters and threw them away as fast as I wrote them.

Finally I decided to take desperate steps, go into town, rent a car and drive up the Millicoma. If he really had gone to Minnesota, I was sunk anyway. If not, I would simply present myself at the door of his little grey home in the West and let him jump to conclusions. I felt sure he would jump to the right conclusions.

Old Fox came up Friday morning to check the dam since

there was danger the freshet might wreck it. Bonny wanted to go to Coos Bay, too, so we asked Old Fox to drive us back with him. And a fine, romantic figure I cut, I thought, sloshing my way to his pickup in raincoat and boots. No perfume, no sheer stockings, no fancy hairdo, none of the little allurements considered de rigueur for an enterprise such as I was undertaking.

"Brace yourselves, girls," Old Fox said. "This is going to be one hell of a trip."

We jounced and slithered our way through miles of chuckholes and oozy mud, our eyes narrowed, leaning forward and peering through a wrinkled curtain of rain. When we reached a bend in the road called Devil's Elbow, Old Fox jammed on the brakes, almost skidding us into the river which ran, swift and dun colored, several hundred feet below. Ahead of us what once had been a road was now a brown hill of mud where the mountain above had given way to the torrents of rain.

"Well, I'll be damned," Old Fox said. "We'll be lucky if we can back out of this loblolly." He threw the pickup into reverse and it slowly struggled backward, while I gripped the seat and stared down into the canyon on my right. It was a quarter mile to the turnaround. We were almost there when the pickup gave a sickening lurch. The wheels turned but the pickup refused to budge.

"All third-class passengers get out and push," Old Fox said, as if he were enjoying himself, the old coot.

Bonny and I scrambled out into mud so deep it came almost to our boot tops. With each of us shoving against a front fender and Old Fox rocking the pickup with the motor revving, the balky thing finally moved and backed slowly away from us. I was glad enough to be walking since the pickup continued to skid and slide all over the road.

Bonny and I were mud splattered and puffing by the time we reached the turnaround where Old Fox waited, and when we got back to camp and slopped our way to the cookhouse stove we dripped all over Lucien's clean kitchen.

I was not only wet, I was also thoroughly discouraged. To start off primed to declare one's love and end up slogging through mud is a terrible comedown.

"I'll go start your oil stoves," Snoozy said, shaking his head disapprovingly. "You get out of them wet clothes before you catch your death of dampness."

"Funny, I'm not a bit wet," Old Fox gloated, and noisily slurped his coffee.

Since we were half frozen, Bonny and I, as a special dispensation, were allowed to put on woolen slacks and sweaters, the permission coming from Lucien rather than Old Fox, who wisely kept out of the discussion, since after all Lucien was boss of the cookhouse. The few men in camp were unlikely to disapprove anyway. They were playing poker all day and most of the night and I suspected they might even forget to come to the cookhouse to eat.

The morning stretched out interminably. We had already polished every inch of the place and all the cookie cans were full. Bonny busied herself trying to learn how to make hollandaise sauce from Lucien, who sat by the stove, stroking his cat and calling out directions. Boygen's eyes were closed and there was a look of rapture on his face.

I wandered over and stared out of the window. A dismal sight. When I went outdoors and stood on the cookhouse porch it looked even less propitious. From my post I could see the two rivers which (along with the mountain behind me) fenced our camp in. The rivers seemed to have risen two feet since we had set out on our unsuccessful drive. For a few minutes I watched their muddy turbulence and then went back into the cookhouse, conscious of a stirring of uneasiness. If you live long enough in that part of the country, you learn what nature can do in the way of floods when she sets her mind to it.

Old Fox still sat opposite Lucien by the stove, cradling the coffee cup in his hands. "What the dickens are you staring out the window for?" he asked.

"I'm trying to figure out a way up that sleazy mountain," I told him.

"Going for a walk this fine day?"

"Not if I can help it," I said. It was a miserable-looking mountain, slippery, soggy and stacked with the rocks, stumps and discarded limbs which make logged-off land such a mess. "The last thing I want is to try that gooey hill," I told him. "And I don't a bit like the idea of rain down my neck all night, under some dripping tree."

Old Fox snorted and I joined him by the stove. "The bridges are sound," he said. "If the rivers get too high, we'll go over to the Power Company's line shack. But there's no danger yet. Those cables will hold till doomsday."

It seemed to me he sounded a little uneasy, just the same. "Well," I said, "I can swim with the best of you. Not fancy, you understand, but I'm built for floating and—" I stopped, listening to the sound of footsteps on the porch and then the voices of Wild Bill and Indian Johnny, back from the dam.

"Well, how about it?" Old Fox asked as the two men walked into the kitchen.

"Okay," Wild Bill said. "We got the gate open in time."

Water was running off their clothes and down their faces. Another man was right behind them.

"Edison!" I yelled.

"So you *are* still here," he said. He was soaking wet and

covered with mud, but to me he looked like an angel appearing straight out of heaven.

"Johnny and I picked him up at the dam," Wild Bill said. "His jeep's on the other side of the slide. We had to leave the half-track five miles down the road."

All three of them went over at once to the dormitory for dry clothes, while Bonny, Lucien and I hurried around getting lunch ready. I was not the least bit worried about the flood any longer. At the moment I did not care if we all went floating off downriver together, as long as Edison and I were in the same ark.

I felt sure Edison had come back to find me. There seemed to be no other reason why he should have slogged all the way up to the Ticoma. Wild Bill, I decided, must have passed the word along about my being in camp, asking desperate questions about him and acting forlorn. Under the circumstances, I expected Edison to stay around the cookhouse after lunch. Well, he did not stay around at all. He went off with the other men and played poker all afternoon.

They all came in again for supper, but immediately afterward rushed back to their poker game, Old Fox with them. When the supper work was done, I sat down in the cookhouse, waiting expectantly. Nobody seemed to want coffee badly enough to leave the game. And I simply could not understand why Edison did not seek me out. There had been romance in his arrival, coming in out of the storm like that, after struggling all the way through mud and slashing rain to reach me. It was in the very finest tradition. Then when he got here all he did was play poker. It was beyond my comprehension.

Finally I gave up and started over to the Old Homestead. When Bonny said she was scared, I was happy enough to have her spend the night with me. I was feeling jittery, too. "Those dumb poker players don't have sense enough to be scared," I grumbled, jumping over puddles and floundering through mud.

Lying in my bed, I could hear the steady whap of the rain. It was a constant undertone to the clapping thunder and the clamorous voice of the river. The river did not sound a bit like the tuneful little stream which had lulled me to sleep all summer. I could hear stones rolling over and over and above that sound, the hiss and roar of waters.

At midnight we were jolted out of our beds by a suddenly intensified clamor. There was piercing, screaming wind and ripping trees, a whole jumble of sounds, like mountains falling in while cymbals crashed.

We both jumped out of bed and opened the door a crack. Since nothing seemed to be falling close by, we stepped onto the porch. At that moment the yard lights went out, leaving total blackness and the terrible noise.

"What is it?" Bonny whispered.

A beam from a flashlight knifed past us and played along the bridge. We could see driftwood piling up against the bridge and hear it groan under the pressure while the cables vibrated with a horrible hissing sound.

"Hey, you," I shouted. "How about throwing the light over toward the back of our cabin?"

The yellow light swerved and for an instant I saw the river cutting its way almost to our cabin's sills.

"Kinda high, isn't it?" Bonny yelled to the anonymous light bearer. No answer.

"What shall we do now, Lee?" she whispered. "Gosh, I'm scared."

"We might as well get these wet things off and go back to bed," I told her. "We're not floating yet and we really can't do a thing until those guys get some sense scared into them. Poker! My gosh."

We had just crawled back into bed when there was a loud knocking at our door. Edison and Wild Bill were out there with a lantern.

"Here, take this," Wild Bill said, shoving the lantern at me. "And get dressed pronto. You can each take one suitcase. We're getting out of here."

At least it was a relief to stop pretending we were not really scared. We scrambled into our clothes and I stuffed my most prized belongings into a bag, while Bonny ran to her cabin to pack. As I lugged my bag past Lucien's cabin he called out to me from the doorway, "Put together some food. I cannot come. I am looking for Boygen."

In the cookhouse, I pulled out two huge kettles and when Bonny came in, we crammed food into them. Coffee and cream, bread and butter, bacon and eggs, cans of ham and corned beef, sugar, canned fruit and cheese. Above the screaming of the storm I heard Lucien's voice calling, "Here, baby. Here, boy."

We dragged out half a sack of potatoes and a full can of cookies. Even if we managed to cross the bridge, we knew we could not get down the road and if we reached the line shack, we would need plenty to eat. "Hurry, hurry," Bonny kept repeating.

Lucien stepped into the kitchen, looking pale in the dim light of the lantern. "Boygen has gone. He requested to go out, only a little moment ago and he has not returned."

"He'll be all right," I said, hoping it was true. "Animals have an instinct about these things."

Lucien stood very straight in soggy pajamas, just inside the door. "I will not leave without Boygen," he announced.

There was the sound of running footsteps and Moonshine

Jake stuck his head in the door. "Wild Bill's going to try to drive across the bridge," he said.

Without bothering about the rain, Bonny and I both raced to the bridge approach where the men were already gathered around the Louse. Its harsh motor sounded no louder than a kitten's purr compared to the howling river. A pile of driftwood, fifteen feet high, stretched upriver behind the bridge as far as the five-cell flashlight could stab the darkness. In spite of screaming wind and hissing river, grating rocks and falling trees, I could hear the booming thud of logs as they joined the jam above.

The bridge, hidden from view by ebony water, squealed in protest and the taut cables, with gurgling eddies around them, vibrated like violin strings.

"You can't go, Bill," Old Fox said. "How in hell do we know there's any planks on that bridge? Heck, there may not even be a bridge there."

"Something's holding back that crap," Wild Bill said, climbing into the Louse.

"Don't let him go!" I screamed and found other people were shouting the same thing.

Old Fox reached over and jerked the key from the ignition. "We're better off in the cookhouse tonight. It's the highest point of ground in camp. When it's daylight, we'll see what's best to do." He turned around and started plodding back to the cookhouse. "Come on, all of you. That's an order, Bill."

We all dragged along behind, while Old Fox grumbled, "Maybe Lucien can make coffee on the son-of-a-bitching heater."

We were a disheveled group, the eleven of us, standing dripping around the heater and willing the coffee water to boil. Lucien had put on his clothes, but his hands were trembling, and every minute or two he would go to the door and call Boygen.

"I've been a damn old fool," Old Fox said, his back to the heater and his stocky legs, as usual, planted belligerently apart. "We ought to have moved over to the line shack this morning. I hated to trespass on co-op property if we didn't have to. Well, I've just been a fool."

"It wasn't your fault, boss," Moonshine Jake told him. "We played poker too darn long, that's all."

"Shucks," Indian Johnny said, "who's afraid of those bitty ole cricks?"

"I am," Old Fox said. "The bridge across the Coila is just as dangerous as this one. Even though there's not much drift against it, there's a jam all right. Probably right around the bend. If either jam goes, we'll have a flash flood in seconds."

The only sound in the dimly lighted room was the sputtering of the oilstove. "Well, folks," Old Fox said, "we may have a fifty-fifty chance of getting out of here with whole skins. If a bridge goes, the current is going to be full of all sorts of junk. It's not going to be easy to get to that blamed hill." He turned around and glanced at me. "You were right, Lee. It's a damn poor place to go for a walk."

I don't know about the others, but my own stomach had a very hollow feeling, although I joined right in as everybody began to talk at once, trying hard to appear unconcerned. I think we all wanted to make Old Fox feel better. All at once the hubbub died abruptly. A pitiful "meow" rose right up from under our feet. Lucien gave a jerk; his hand with the coffee cup stopped in midair. Then the cup clattered to the floor. He grabbed the lantern and limped to the far end of the porch, the rest of us at his heels. I could see him holding the lantern high and staring despairingly down at the rising water, which already had reached the cookhouse stringers. It was no longer humanly possible to get under the cookhouse where Boygen was stranded on some sill.

"Maybe the water won't get any higher," Snoozy suggested.

Lucien gave him one look, terrible in its misery and then, as the cat cried again, he covered his ears with his hands and limped off to his own cabin. The rest of us went back into the cookhouse. There seemed to be nothing else we could do. The wretched meowing grew louder.

"I've had enough of this!" Edison exploded. "Why can't we tear the blamed floor up? I'm going after some tools."

"You'll have to wade or swim," Bill called after him, then grabbed the flashlight and followed him out of the back door. They were back in minutes, drenched to the skin, their arms full of crowbars, saws and hammers, and I jumped up and rushed over to get Lucien, running along the high plank to his cabin and bursting through the door without knocking.

Lucien sat slumped in his rocker, a thick bath towel tied around his head, to drown out the kitten's cry, and two huge diamonds on his hand, probably the only tangible things he had to show for long years in many kitchens.

"Come on!" I cried. "Quick! The boys are going to tear up the floor."

Lucien's whole face came alive in one second. He started limping for the door and I grabbed his coat and threw it over his shoulders. I could hardly keep up with him on the way back. The boys already had the floorboards torn up and were sawing away at the subfloor. Boygen was still crying. It must have seemed to the poor kitten as if he were being attacked from above, too. When Edison and Bill finally got up two boards of the subfloor, Edison reached under and pulled out the bedraggled and terrified cat, which he handed to Lucien. The old man sat down suddenly on a bench and shut his eyes tight for an instant, while Bonny and I hurried off to get some kitchen towels. By the time the kitten had been rubbed dry, it was purring as contentedly as if nothing unfortunate had ever happened to it.

The night went on endlessly. The heater was circled with benches where we had all been trying to dry out. At one point Snoozy put on hip boots and brought an armload of blankets from the commissary, but they did little to soften the benches. We were all waiting for the same sound, the boom of a bridge's collapse or the roar of a jam going out. When anyone, looking for a snack, happened to slam a cupboard door, we all jumped. I found myself thinking of Mother and Dad. I had drifted away from their religion but still I hoped Dad had not dropped to sleep that night before family worship. The prayer always ended the same way: "Bless all our children wherever they are and keep them safe."

A few hardy souls tried to sleep, stretched out on a bench. Snoozy and Indian Johnny and two young loggers cleared the setups from a table and played pinochle, the flickering gas lantern highlighting the rough hands holding the cards. I kept trying to get Edison's eye, but he was deeply involved in a discussion of trout flies with Old Fox, so finally I dozed off.

Morning came with the rain unabated. We seemed to be floating in the middle of a muddy, churning lake. The water was halfway up the other buildings and the powerhouse had disappeared completely. The men got shovels and set out to cut steps up the miserable mountain.

"The hell with it," Wild Bill yelled after them. "What

good's it going to do us to climb Pneumonia Hill anyway?" He turned and scowled at Old Fox. "All right, boss. Do you give me the key to the Louse or do I beat hell out of you?"

Silently, Old Fox handed the keys to Bill.

"Hey, you guys," Bill said to the two young loggers, "get your pike poles. One of you ride each front fender. Johnny, you can wade ahead. Now test every foot of the way with your pikes, see? We don't want to lose this Louse in any goddamn hole. Come on, Ed, you ride with me. Let's leave the doors open."

The sturdy high-wheeled jeep, standing in three feet of water, coughed a couple of times, and then settled down to a steady clatter.

Bonny and I watched from the cookhouse windows as it inched its way across the hidden bridge. Johnny and the boys on the front fenders tested each plank with the long poles. The planks were still in place. After an eternity of waiting, the Louse conquered the first bridge. There still remained the floodwater between the bridges, hiding the place where the road was supposed to be. It was over three feet deep and dotted with swiftly gliding logs. Even if the Louse's motor did not die from wetness, it could get whanged by a wild log. I saw Indian Johnny, who had been wading, get up in back of the Louse, his apparent purpose being to deflect any runaway log which might attack from the rear.

The second bridge was also intact. They reached the other side safely, but there, when they attempted to turn around, the Louse stuck. We could see the men struggling to push it, and after a few moments, the plucky little jeep climbed out of the hole and headed back.

"Okay, folks," Old Fox said. "Let's go."

We all ran out and as the jeep sloshed up we loaded it

with food and our bags. Although the rain had not let up, the water had stopped rising, which could only mean it was backing up ominously behind the driftwood. It was certainly now or never.

Lucien got in back with Boygen in his arms and Bonny and I climbed in front with Wild Bill. This time Edison and Indian Johnny rode the front fenders with the pike poles and a husky young logger the back bumper. There were eleven people in or on the Louse and nobody knew if the added weight would be the last straw which would break the bridge's back or not.

Slowly Wild Bill eased the Louse out onto the bridge. We could feel the bridge sway as we inched across it and the noise, now that we were in the middle of the river, was deafening. Finally the Louse gave a lurch and we knew we were on land again. But the water was even deeper.

"It's right up to the motor," Bill told us. "Hang tight, gals."

We rocked our way through the swift water while logs and debris danced all around us. The Louse actually leaped to get onto the second bridge. From there we could see the beginning of the jam on the Coila, just around the bend, as Old Fox had surmised. Below the drift, the river was still picking up debris from its widening banks and a beaver was swimming rapidly away. Probably the freshet had wrecked his home, too.

As we crept carefully along the second bridge, I began to think safety was within easy reach. And then, suddenly, without warning, a deadhead which had been caught against the bridge, upended and fairly pounced on the struggling Louse. It caught it on the rear bumper and with a sickening lurch, the Louse stopped with one rear wheel over the side of the bridge.

No one said a word for an instant. We sat stiff with tightened throats while the deadhead went on its topsy-turvy way downstream. Then Edison and Indian Johnny stepped cautiously off the fenders and, jamming their pike poles into the bridge planks, held against the jeep.

Old Fox slid open the panel in back of us. "What do we do now, Bill?" he asked softly, as if even a loud voice might start us rolling off the bridge.

"There's the winch. If we can just stay right side up—"

"By God, the winch! That's right. Who's man enough to get that cable across the river and choke a stump with it?" he yelled, forgetting his caution in the excitement.

"Ed and I'll go," Indian Johnny yelled back. "We're the strongest." It did not sound a bit like bragging, either.

"Let me go, too, boss," Moonshine Jake begged.

"You stay here. Nothing but your two eyes would be showing above that mess of water." Old Fox was himself again, now that there were plans to make and orders to bark. He pointed at the two young loggers. "You two get ahold of those pike poles so Ed and Johnny can let loose of them."

"Easy, Bill. Loosen her up," Johnny ordered as he and Edison took hold of the cable. "We cain't haul this critter outa here by ourselves."

Slowly the two cable bearers started out, fighting every step of the way to retain their footing, while I kept saying under my breath, "Please, please, don't slip."

"I can't see a stump near," Snoozy said.

"That myrtle tree," Old Fox shouted. "Try that, boys."

It would have been impossible for the struggling pair to hear, but they headed for the myrtle tree anyway and finally succeeded in getting the cable choked around its base. Edison gave the signal to "go ahead on her" and with great caution Wild Bill threw the lever into gear that wound the cable in. Slowly the cable grew taut and began to lift us. With a lurch the Louse jumped back onto the bridge and slowly rocked and splashed its way toward the bank, like a duck waddling through tall grass.

"You suppose you can make it along the hillside, if we land downriver a ways?" Wild Bill asked. "That myrtle tree isn't exactly on the path."

"Just lead us to some good solid earth and you'll see," Bonny squealed happily.

Like a little army of drowned rats we all staggered along the hillside. Bonny and I were each carrying a purse, a bag and, for heaven's sake, a folded umbrella. Bonny had a big, very wet Teddy bear under one arm and I carried the music box Gina had given me. The men were loaded down with cans and kettles of food and their own gear. Lucien brought up the rear, Boygen riding safely under his coat.

The co-op cabin stood a dozen feet above the flood line, its foundations on good solid earth. We all went trooping in, staring around the roomy cabin with its rusty stoves and roughhewn walls as if we never had seen anything so fine before. I noticed that the co-op boys had left a pile of nice dry wood, too.

Everybody seemed to feel just as gay and lighthearted all of a sudden as I did. Even the homely, ordinary jobs were a wonderful joy, the building of rousing fires in both wood-burning stoves, the frying of spuds and bacon and eggs, the making of hot biscuits and gravy and coffee.

When the dishes were washed and put away, we all went back to stove-hugging again, pulling up as close as we could to the lovely fire, until a crash, louder than anything the night before, brought us out of our seats and sent us rushing to the windows. The Ticoma bridge had gone out.

"Look!" Bonny yelled. "The cookhouse is moving!"

In the midst of all the jam's debris, I could see the cookhouse moving sedately out into the swifter water. Once in the main river, it whirled giddily around twice, the roof caved in and table and benches went bouncing along among runaway logs, uprooted trees, bark and stumps. All sweeping downriver. Out of my life.

Edison was standing right behind me, but he was not looking at me. He was looking out at the wild river, his face a little worn and tired after the long night.

Out of my life, I thought forlornly. And then I noticed my thumbs. My hands were clasped in front of me, fat little thumbs uppermost, looking perfectly capable of handling any situation. I could have sworn the little rascals were signaling to me.

"Edison," I said and then stopped. There is no sense in explanations, I thought. Oh well, maybe sometime. But not now. "Edison," I began again, in a loud, firm voice, "do you still have that bottle of champagne?"

"I sure have," he said.

"Well, when we get out of here, let's have a celebration. At your tree farm." I glanced up at him to make sure he knew what I was talking about. He knew all right. He gave me the sweetest smile I have ever seen on a human face. "I mean," I hurried on, "if you still want to?"

"Sure do," he said, and I leaned back against the wall with a sigh. Let the waters roar. Let the rains slash down, I felt really secure for the first time in my life.

We hope you enjoyed this title from Echo Point Books & Media

Visit our website to see our full catalog and take 10% off your order total at checkout!

An Aviator's Wife
Adelaide Ovington

In this memoir, Adelaide captures the flavor of the times, paints a vivid portrait of her marriage, and provides a lively account of Earle Ovington's early aviation adventures.

Arctic Adventure
Peter Freuchen

In this memoir, Freuchen writes about the Inuit with genuine respect and affection, describing their stoicism amidst hardship, their spiritual beliefs, their ingenious methods of surviving their harsh environment, and their humor and joy in the face of danger and difficulties.

Extraordinary Zen Masters
John Stevens

Stephens tells the stories of Ikkyu, Hakuin, and Ryokan. These are three of the greatest Zen masters in history—each unique, each an outstanding artist, and each a teacher of future generations. The biographies of these three men are full of insight on leading a meaningful life.

The Marathon Monks of Mount Hiei
John Stevens

Steves offers a glimpse into the seven-year training period for these "running buddhas," who figuratively circle the globe on foot. During one incredible 100-day stretch, they cover 52.5 miles daily. The prize they seek to capture is the greatest thing a human being can achieve: enlightenment in the here and now.

Rengetsu: Life and Poetry of Lotus Moon
Biography & Translation by John Stevens

As a poet, potter, painter, martial artist, and Buddhist nun, Otagaki Rengetsu transformed a life of tragedy into one of artistic and spiritual transcendence as one of Japan's greatest female poets. Stevens captures the radiant simplicity of Rengetsu's life in this biography and new translation of her work.

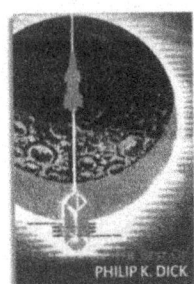

The Best of Philip K. Dick
Philip K. Dick

Philip K. Dick didn't predict the future— he summoned the desperate bleakness of our present directly from his fevered paranoia. Collected here are thirteen of his most Dickian tales, funhouse realities with trap doors and hidden compartments, the literary equivalent of optical illusions, tricks of perspective.

Buy direct and save 10% at www.EchoPointBooks.com

DISCOUNT CODE: WOODS

www.ingramcontent.com/pod-product-compliance
Lightning Source LLC
Chambersburg PA
CBHW080637170426
43200CB00015B/2868